# A Journey Of

A discovery of self and the life that is living
through us all

## SANJEEV KUMAR

Copyright © 2019 Sanjeev Kumar
All rights reserved.

# **DEDICATION**

Dedicated to all my fellow human beings, who are among the living. And to those, who we have lost, I hope they lived well.

Thank you......

# CONTENTS

# ACKNOWLEDGMENTS

Thankful to all those special people, who somehow developed a liking for whatever I write and share. And after publishing my first book titled " Poems of Self Discovery " ( available on Amazon ). I realised, it's probably worth writing another book. But this time as a compilation of poems, thoughts, imaginations and everything in between. Describing the journey inside of a human mind. The book is a product of my own journey in life and the continuous self reflection.

We learn from each other, and life is always the best teacher. No one is ever born with a manual on how to live a human life. Living, as I understand from my own journey so far is, mostly about trial & error. You have to learn to be your own anchor and also be your best hope. We had no say in our own creation, and we find ourself living. And live we all must that I know, but how, is what I am trying to figure out.

So my best wishes to you all, for your journey ahead. Go gentle and be gentle to yourself. A life is living you, and somehow living always get in the way of life.

# 1POEMS

# 2 A MUSEUM...

*A museum ...*


I was a museum once
Stored inside me
Was my history

A history that
I thought was me
It made me
Whoever I thought, I was

There was a certain mystery
To my being the museum

I didn't know what
I was carrying in me

Rusting away was my humanity
There was a constant struggle
As I felt the need
To preserve my individuality

I was an individual
My life was my own
Yet I had
No control over
What I was sold

I had a heritage
The culture of my ancestors
Was also quite strong
That is what I was told
To continue and carry on

I realised that
My individuality didn't
Come from me
But a story of old

A story that
I didn't write
So I took it all
As I was told

The collection was not mine
It was a history of old

Search I did
Of who I maybe
Then I felt
I was getting old

Museum is not
What I will be

So I broke away
And we separated
From the museum of old
Where I didn't feel
I was ever whole

# 3 YOU ARE YOUR AUTHOR AND YOUR PRIEST...

# You are your author and your priest...

Sometimes you need people detox
Just you with you
And none of the
Humans made rules

Be a messenger
To yourself with no message
A preacher to yourself
But with nothing to preach

A dreamer with no goal or aim
Yes, you can hear loud and clear
All what the human society is
Or could become but then
You have nothing to complain

Be free and not a slave
To an idea or the rules

Don't live because
A God made you
Live, because a Life
Is living you, through you
As it is through a tree

Being a human
Shouldn't be a curse
Where all you do is rust

Chipping away your peace

Because you want to
Seek glory and feast

The sky above you is
Not always clear and blue
Clouds and the fog will
Make your world look dark

But sometimes you will need
To learn to appreciate the dark
Only then your mind will find
A way to see through it all

Free yourself from
The fear of the unknown
You know, the world was
Unknown to you
Before your were born

And whatever you have learnt
To hold dear, will all be gone

As you will learn to live
You may come to believe
That You are your author
And your priest

4 HOPE ......

Hope.....


Learn to live today
To the best you can
Try you may
All you can

But no one can borrow
Their own tomorrow

Live before you die
Grow as a rye

Heaven is inside you
And so is hell, you know

The dark ally
In your mind
Will take you away
And your soul

You fight through the day
Try to keep your
Troubles at bay

Sometimes there is no time
You may feel
If only you
Could ask a divine
To tell you that
Everything will be fine

Remember, to not surrender
Yes! there will be thunder

Hope is your dope
And it is also your rope

Grab it, you must
As tight as you can
Until the day
You learn to
Find your way

# 5 IS THERE A MESSAGE ...

Is there a message ...


Silence is what
I want to feel
And silence is what
I feel, I would like to be

No song to sing
The words can't say
What I want them to mean

A journey to nowhere
Suddenly feels as
A journey should be

Lost inside my mind
Some may say, I maybe
But the question I ask is
What if, that is where
I may want to be

The future of past is
Not a mystery
It will be
What some of us
Would  want it to be

History is a story we write
To tell others
How things were

The story of past
Is a not always narrated
As a matter of fact

It may so happen
When nothing you
May want, will seem to happen

But the life you are
Learns to live
And goes on
Even if it fails to please

Moments of magic
You always seek
While living is
Never the life's main theme

And sometimes nothing is
As it may seem

So you may ask
What is my task
And is there a message
Or is something guiding me
To a certain destiny

# 6 TRAJECTORY OF HUMAN HISTORY

# Trajectory of human history...

The peace that I seek
Is probably in me
And the same
Goes for the happiness, I feel

At times when
We are weak
And uncertain of
What will be
We tend to worry
Down to our heels

Maybe I will come through
Or is this it?
Wondering if this is
How it is

A story of life
That we all
Try to live

And at times the journey
May feel lonely
But that's when
You also learn to know

That it is how
We all learn and grow
And become the person
We are, and will be

This is the trajectory
Of most humans history

Peace and happiness is
The seed you sow
In a fertile mind
That is yours

Which may help you grow
And one day reap
The rewards of what
You once sowed

# Time for a BREAK ?

Hope you enjoyed the five poems, and maybe it's time for some self reflection ? And if that's what you feel like doing then, please do jot down your thoughts on the empty page. To continue reading, please turn to the next page.

Thank you ....

( This page is left empty for your notes )

# 7 LOST TO THE DARK

## Lost to the dark...

The Sun don't shine
In the dark
Sometimes you may
Find yourself sitting
On your own
In a park

Your mind maybe going through
A phase of self reflection
Going over every detail and detection

You may want to
Shine light on the dark corners
That you cannot see

But light that you seek
Has to travel through the dark
And at times
An object can
Block its path

The light reflected
By an object
Is what helps you see

And not all object can
Emit their own light, you see

So it must reflect
The beam in order

For it to be seen

The universe that you see
Was once much brighter
And everything in it
Was tucked in tighter

Then things started drifting apart
And there will come a time
When the night sky
Will all be dark

The  galaxies and the stars
Will have all moved far apart
Leaving the space in
Between them all dark

You may learn to see yourself
Through others' reflection
And how you see others
Will reflect your own perception

It is people who
Help you shine bright
And it is people
Who will leave
You in the dark

And if you drift apart then
Whatever you had and were
Will all be
Lost to the dark

8 YOU IN ME....

# You in me....

The fear is not
That I will die one day

I hope, I will have the chance
To say goodbye

You were to good to me
Now I know
The good in you
Saw the good in me

You saw what
I couldn't see
But then I didn't know
What was ME

The moon and the stars
They all love me

Because that's how
I see them
And that's how I want them
To see me

You came to me
Or life found you
All that, I don't know

But thanks for being
Who you were to me

The you in me
Is going strong

And for all I know
It may live on

# 9 DISCONNECTED ......

## Disconnected....

Wondering inside my head I was
Heading somewhere or so I thought
I couldn't find a direction of
Where I was

Questions were many
And questions are all
What I had

Is it a phase
Or am I just sad

No no, said a voice
In my head
It can't be that bad

Do I need to exist, I asked
The world is not what I need
But not because I feel it's bad

It has hunger
And it has pain
Also the glory
And the rain

Some survive, and some don't
You may say then
Is there something wrong

I have been to places

I didn't know
And I have heard of stories
You may not know

Connect the dots
Is what I have done
The dots are many
And so is the connection

Some may say
The connection is
What you need
And it maybe indeed
It is on what
The society feeds

But why is our connection so weak
That we need it to be constantly tweaked

Is it the world
Or is it just who we are

Disconnected with those
Who are our own
Because of the way
We are Conditioned and grown

# 10 SAYING WHAT YOU HAVE TO SAY ...

## Saying what you have to say...

They said, you speak not of
What is deemed acceptable
The society knows
What is best

Racist and bigoted is
What you may become
If you speak of
What is not politically correct

Silence those who can speak freely
And grant them no liberty

Speak not what's in your mind
But speak of what
You are allowed to say

And that is just
The social justice of today

We are a free society, you see
And left and right
Are the only two ways
It can be

If you are not with me
Then you are against me, some say
What was right once
Is wrong today

Little did I know
That I was born to be a slave

But to please you
With what I will say
Is not the reason
For my stay

So long my friend, so long
This is not the day
For me to stop you
From whatever you want to say

I will quit the day
When you will have no say
The society is not free
If you can't pray

The speaker will hear you now
So you can speak your piece
And even if that piece
May disturb my peace

Say what you have to say
The debate and the hate
Is all part of the freedom
And it is here to stay

A freedom to freely co exist
With those who may or may not agree
It is how we
Learn to be free

Next page ..

# 11 SHE ...

## SHE...

I looked for light
In the emptiness
Of darkness, she said

The Ocean felt dark
And so was her life, it seemed
Her heart was heavy
With sorrow and sadness

She tried, and she tried hard
To be happy, and just to be
But nothing worked
As far as she could see

A hero is what
She was looking for
A saviour to catch her
In her free fall

And catch her, no one did
So she thought, she was done
Life was no more fun
Drowning in her own darkness, she was

Slowly passing away
Almost as if
She was dying everyday

That's her story so far
But it is not how
She should end

Start a fresh, she should
Burn the darkness
As the fuel
To light her way
Up to the hill

Dream away, I say
And on the way
You may learn to know
That your hero and saviour
Was always you

Do it, and do it
Not just for you
But for the she
Who maybe you

## Time for a BREAK ?

I have always been quite curious about how people learn to relate to each other. Hope you enjoyed the ten poems. And I wonder if you were able to relate to the poems, at all ?. If you did then, please do jot down your thoughts on the empty page.  And to continue reading, please turn to the next page.

By the way, we are taking a break from poetry in the next section. I thought it will be a good change.

Thank you ....

( This page is left empty for your notes )

# 12 THE MORNING MUSINGS..

# 13 MY ROMANCE WITH LIVING AND LIFE..

# My romance with living and life

One day while rushing for an early morning meeting, I bumped into an old friend who I haven't seen for years. We exchanged greetings, and agreed to catch up soon over a drink. I got in the tube (metro), and was on my way to the meeting. It is then I remembered that, I may not have his contact details on my new phone. But before I could search for his contact details, I saw a text come through saying " Oh! Forget to you tell, my father has been diagnosed with dementia ", and that got me thinking.

Sometimes you create memories, so you can cherish them later, yet there is always a possibility that you may not be able to recall all those memories. And not just the memories, but also who you were. I am assuming that, most of us would have heard of people, who are going through it, and you keep hoping that it won't happen to you. And I sincerely hope that it doesn't. Anyways, so the takeaway for me is, maybe I shouldn't live for memories or a legacy. And why would you, if you one day, you won't be able to remember any of it ?

Living for me is about, letting a life live through me to its full potential, whatever it might be. And getting fully immersed in the moment and the overall experience. Because who knows, one day I may not even remember, or be able to recall those moments of magic that made living a worthy experience. Therefore creating memories is probably not my way of letting a life live through me.

I have realised that, for me, it's about the experience of living and letting go. Because nothing is mine, not even my identity. I wasn't born with it, and no one ever is. I have learnt to be who I am, and I could have easily been someone else. And it is when my mind somehow started to learn to let go of whatever it thought, it was or had, or wanted to be. That's when I started my romance with living and life.

# 14 A SIGN FROM THE UNIVERSE...

# A sign from the Universe ?

It is while having my dinner, the mind that is me was exploring a thought. And Part of it was related to a conversation I had with someone I know. I realised that, I wasn't getting anywhere so decided to go to bed instead. Little did I know that the idea will still be bugging me in the morning.

And in the morning when I was having a shower I started wondering, is there a way of knowing that, somehow we are or maybe, getting a guidance from the Universe without releasing it? Sounds quite stupid and unscientific, isn't it, but is it ? So I thought, let's try to explore the possibility.

The question I asked myself is, why do we humans do whatever we do. For example, we have created religions, societies under one nation states, and then within societies there are sub societies. Many different languages, and the list goes on. There are those of us who crave power and dominance. Why do we do all this ? Is it in our nature ? And then my mind somehow wanted to find a similar reference in Nature here on Earth and the bigger Universe. To see, if there is a comparison.

So what do we see ? Well! from what we know so far of our universe, the universe has unlimited diversity within it, starting with different galaxies, Stars and solar systems. Pockets of space which are just empty, followed by galaxies packed with powerful objects like super massive black holes among others. Also within the universe, energy and gravity are in a constant struggle for dominance. And the overall picture of our Universe is quite chaotic. There is nothing harmonious about the Universe.

And then, let us look at, what the nature has built here on Earth. Starting with  magnificent tall mountains and the list goes on. As I see it, our ancestors have tried to simply mimic or in other words imitate nature and the universe at large. Possibly without knowing that they were doing so. We build tall mega buildings to show our strength and might. The societies and nation states that we have created for ourselves are, to some extent quite comparable to different galaxies and star system in our Universe. We carry the tendency to awe others with whatever we feel is our strength. Also, we continue to carry forward, what the psychologists call, the costly signal that, we picked up from our animal friends. To awe and win over our preferred sexual partners, by showing them our strengths, be it our wealth or intelligence etc.

So in all, aren't we just mimicking or playing out, what we see around us in the bigger Universe as well as nature here on Earth. We are carrying all these information without consciously realising it, but enacting then nevertheless. It's fun, isn't it ?

# 15 A FALSE NARRATIVE....

# A false narrative

The question I ask myself is, why do we embrace or buy into the established understanding of a subject matter without ever questioning the assumptions based on which those understandings were developed at the time. It's probably how we have been conditioned by the society. But as the modern human society continues to evolve, with it comes learning and unlearning. And therefore, the assumptions of yesteryears may not be relevant today at all. This is why I feel that it is important for us, to continue to question the old narratives.

And it is exactly what I intend to do, by taking a risk to discuss a subject that somehow creates a bit of unease inside our society, and yet it gets discussed quite often, but as a repeat of the same old, as some would say.

So to begin with, let's have a clarity that, both men and women are indeed equal. But also different, in terms of their physiology. Men and women are equal part of the same human race. So then, what's the issue ? Well! In my view, the unresolved issues have roots in the assumptions made by our forefathers. For whatever reason, some men, who played a dominant role in shaping the society of the time, probably concluded that, a woman to them was also the pleasure provider, and women's body thereafter became the ultimate pleasure tool for most men, at the time. I won't go into the physiology or biology, but in short, there are reasons as to why a woman's body or a human body for that matter is so sensual and appealing. And a lot has to do with nature wanting the humans to reproduce. Nature has hard wired humans to have a liking for shape and beauty. And our natural instincts are all by design. These instincts or urges can sometimes be overwhelming, as well as addictive, especially if, they are related to pleasure. And since Women's body got defined as the ultimate pleasure provider, and an asset to own. There was a instinctive need to probably take ownership over it.

And rules got created to control and create a leverage on the Woman. I would suggest, it could possibly be, one of the key reasons why even religious literatures also got into defining the role of a woman, and what she should wear or could do etc. The need to have some degree of control was ever present, and it got reflected in what a society expected from a woman. And some women also knew the power they had over men, so it wasn't at all difficult for them to control the needy also. So somehow both the needy and the owners of pleasure have fought to gain advantage. I do appreciate that, it is entirely a new perspective, and some may argue that it doesn't necessarily accurately reflect the reality. And that's fine. But the question I ask is, what's next ?

There are a number of ways to address address the issue. But the society will need to decide, which one makes better sense. For example, with the help of technology, creating a 100 times more sensual pleasuring tool isn't going to be a problem one day, and in the next 10-15 years, these tools could possibly be commercially available. Also, a human will be able to create another human without the need of impregnating a woman. So the question is, will all this change the role of men and women in the society ? Or make both the genders more equal? Most likely not. Because, as I see it, equality is inside our minds, and if in our minds, we haven't learnt to treat each other as equals then, we are simply discussing a false narrative, aren't we ?

# 16 LOOKING AT SCIENCE AS AN UPGRADE TO RELIGION, AND NOT AS A REPLACEMENT FOR GOD...

## <u>Looking at Science as an upgrade to religion,</u>
## <u>and not as a replacement for God</u>

There is an ongoing debate about science and religion, and it's been on for quite a while now.  My own sense is that, the narrative on both sides somehow fails to marry the two points of view, and the discussions therefore tends to focus on one versus the other. But it doesn't have to be, maybe there is a need for a new perspective ? And with that in mind, I am taking the liberty of sharing my own thoughts on the subject matter, as a part of my contribution to the conversation.

So based on the current theory, everything in the universe and everything the universe is all thanks to quantum fluctuations. And without Werner Heisenberg's uncertainty principle, we will fail to explain away the workings of nature.

In other words, there is no 100% emptiness, and quantum fluctuations can create something from nothing, more or less. Because even in nothing, there is a process which leads to creation of particles and anti particles as virtual pairs, and that's the best theory we have today, as a way to explain how the universe came about. This theory is now part of the establishment and the status quo, but being the idiot that I am. I do struggle with parts of this current theory. And it's one of the reasons why, I would love to figure out, how to create nature. What if the entire system is designed ?

The light ( photons ) from the visible universe that we can see, has had to travel for millions and billion of years, to reach our eyes and instruments that we have created. In other words, they carry an image of the universe before the humans or the earth existed. So we don't really know what's there now. What we see is just a glimpse of a very distant past. And just how does that compare to a human, if at all?

I believe, if we did try to describe the universe in a human context then, it's not that difficult to see or find similarities between the two. And one could also argue that humans do carry traits of what the universe is, in fact, we are part and parcel of whatever the universe is. It is one of the reasons why, I have learnt to appreciate what possibly got our ancestors tempted into the idea of a God, and that God creating humans in the God's image. I know that I struggle quite badly, to buy into the description of a God or the idea of creation in general, as described by religion. But then at the time when, we didn't know or had any other way to understand or explain things around us, the ideas that become part of religious literature was probably the only way, to make sense of everything. And then later science came along.

As I see it, science was an upgrade to religion, but since we humans always tend to push back against change, most of us struggled to fully accept or embrace, the new way of looking at the world around us. Also people of science didn't have to offer a choice between the new idea and the old idea that was religion. Through science, we can explain, why we humans are inherently designed to believe in a concept of God. Also science isn't a replacement for the concept of God, not at all. It is just a new approach, in a way an upgrade to the old way of seeing things.

Like religion, science also requires people to believe in it, or else it won't work. We believe in laws of nature, because we can see it at work. But the idea that, you don't have to believe in God because you can't see that God is quite unscientific, as there are many things around us that we can't see. And for what we can't see or observe, we tend to use our imaginations to visualise it, and then find a way to see or find the evidence for it or dismiss it for that matter. That's how science has evolved.

The only thing we know is that, we don't know much. However as humans, who are nothing but a very tiny cell among trillions of cells, or another way to explain it will be, to see ourselves as a single granule of sand within a pile of unlimited amount of sand. I believe that, we have done remarkably well to be where we are, in terms of not only becoming aware of ourselves and the universe, but also trying to explain away its existence.

# 17 RIGHT TO OWNERSHIP...

## Right to ownership

Over time as HUMANS evolved, we learnt many things and developed various ideas as well as concepts. And quite clearly, besides the idea of religion; money; society ; nation states or Kingdom etc, one of the most important concept that kicked started the market economy as we know it today, was the idea of " right to ownership ".

And by developing this " right of ownership " concept. Humans learnt to claim ownership over the lands as well as natural resources including of water, minerals among other things. And today, Humanity has almost convinced itself that somehow, it has the ownership of Earth. But here is a technical question, do we have an agreement with EARTH, whereby, the Earth wilfully agreed to pass over the ownership of its resources including lands etc to HUMANS ? Well, the answer to that is a BIG No, we don't have such agreement.

So basically, we have convinced ourselves that somehow we are the rightful owners of the land as well as natural resources that quite frankly HUMANS didn't create. And since none of other species sharing the planet have protested against our claim, we have carried on as owners.

And using the same principles, humans learnt to claim exclusivity over GOD or GODS through a concept called " Religion ", where each  religion claims ownership or exclusivity over GOD, but none of these religions have a legally binding agreement with a GOD or GODS, to represent  that GOD. And since the GODS haven't protested, we have carried on with the practice.

So in short, humans are quite good at creating concepts and ideas, and there is nothing wrong with that at all, as long as there are proper disclosures attached to it, and it is not then used as a tool, to enslave humans.

# 18 THE REAL MEANING OF BEING SELFLESS AND LETTING GO...

# The real meaning of being selfless and letting Go

Science tells us that, all the energy available in our universe today was created at the time of Big Bang, and the level of energy has always remained the same throughout the 13.7 billion years of existence of the universe in its current shape and form. The universe is, in a way, the most efficient recycle system there is, so the system has been sustainable, and works quite well.

The basic building block of everything in our universe that we can see and touch, apart from dark matter is an " atom ". It is what makes things in our universe, including us humans. So you can use an atom to make endless number of things. This is what makes the recycling process of the universe work like a clock. The atom that created me was used by the universe to create something else before me, and this process will go on until a day when that atom will get ripped apart by dark energy. But in the billion or trillion plus years life span of an atom, it would have created a million things, including me.

In short, what we are today is, an outcome of a recycling process over which we have no control. The same atom that made me, might have also made a tree; a rock; an animal, a human being among many other things before me. It is estimated that around 37.2 trillion cells are responsible for creating a healthy human body, and everyday millions of them die off, but get replaced by cells that are constantly reproducing. However with age, our body reaches a point where the reproduction and divisions of cell slows down, resulting in our death. But nevertheless the cell has fulfilled its purpose, it works the same way for every human being, good or bad. It has no bias or no favourite, it has a job and it does it well. A cell or an atom never tries to claim an ownership over what it has created, it is also not bothered about appreciation or lack of it. So when you go down to the level of a single atom, you begin to understand, what's the real meaning of being selfless and letting GO.

# 19 CONDITIONING OF A HUMAN MIND...

# Conditioning of a human mind

Who we are, and what becomes of us, to a large extent depends on our training, in other words conditioning. As humans evolved, and learnt to create societies, we realised that ,there needs to be a common glue to bind people together. And that started the process of conditioning.

Every human society has been built on conditioning, and the process requires creating a narrative, whatever that might be. Humans have used tools like the idea of a religion; culture; Gods, and nation states etc, as a way to condition the society.

By and large, this process still continues. Whether the society is a democracy or an autocracy. Without conditioning, it may disintegrate. And all this is fine, but I will encourage my fellow humans, to learn to look at the bigger picture. Because I feel that, we are approaching a time in modern human history where, old tools like the idea of using religion; culture or nation state etc, to condition a human society isn't working well, and is in fact creating a lot of internal conflicts. So we will have to make a very deliberate choice. Do we continue with old conditioning and deal with it's side effects, or find a way to bind the entire human society using the narrative of " Humanity " ?

As I see it, the time is now. Humans have paid a very heavy price, and continue to do so. The side effects, be it hate, mistrust and so on and so forth is, already dangerously disrupting the society. So won't it be nice, if all of us made a deliberate decision to move forward, and voluntarily agreed, to start conditioning the society of tomorrow, based on human values and the evolving ideas of what we call " humanity ". A human is, who we all are, and a human is, who we should be, nothing less and nothing more.

# 20 REST IN PEACE...

# Rest in Peace (R.I.P)

So why does one needs to die, to find peace and rest in peace. I see many of my fellow human beings wishing the dead, rest in peace or as they prefer to write " RIP ". And I wonder if, we have convinced ourselves that, one cannot find peace while being among the livings. Also, does it matter to a dead, if they are resting in peace or not ? And why is it that, only through death, one can find peace ? Is it because, our society and those living among us are incapable of finding peace or living in peace with each other ? What is peace, a state of mind ? I wonder if, we understand who we really are ? A dead has no voice, and to find peace, you don't have to be dead. To understand and appreciate peace, you need to experience it while you are among the living, because when you are dead, nothing matters. Your peace is always inside your own mind, and how you find it is entirely up to you. The way you see the world always reflects your own state of mind, you don't like people, you like them for what you see in them. Your Gods also reflects who you are, and so does your society. Find yourself and your peace before you die, and don't wait for others to wish that, you rest in peace only after your death. That is what, I intend to do.

# 21 WHAT IS A STUPID...

# What is a stupid ?

The grandMa says, a lion is always born a lion, because that it's species. But it takes some time for that lion to realise that, it's a lion. And whether or not that lion behaves like a typical lion would, the perception of that lion being a lion, serves him well in the jungle. A stupid is not born a stupid, but it generally fails to realise that, it is stupid. And while intelligence knows that it has limits, stupidity has no limits. It also fails to comprehend that, it will get discovered that it's stupid. But what is stupid or stupidity ? Is it the lack of intelligence or common sense ? It is probably neither, it is the lack of realisation that one lacks intelligence and common sense or logic.

# 22 LESSON FROM THE POOP...

# Lessons from the Poop

The poop smells only when you have pooped it out. It doesn't, when it is still inside the body. A poop can tell a lot about your health and well-being. And the same goes for your thoughts. If your thoughts stinks then, in a way, it is also telling the world about you and your mental health. To have a good poop, you need to take care of your daily intake, thereby maintaining a good digestive system. And to have good thoughts, you will need a daily intake of good feed. Through the words you speak or write, you do reveal to the world a lot about you and the state of your mind. You can display a beautiful body, but displaying a beautiful mind isn't that easy. Garbage-in will only result in Garbage-out, that's the GiGo affect. We exercise, to keep our body fit, but isn't mind, a part of the body? Physical exercise has benefits, but learning to create positive and beautiful thoughts, makes our minds and the person we become, beautiful forever. So don't we also need to work on our minds to keep it fit ? We all live and experience our lives inside our minds. And the journey to creating a beautiful life worth living, starts inside our mind. Mind is an important tool that makes us who we are, so we need to learn to use it well. But no one is born with a manual, so it's all about trial & error. And that's how we all learn.

## 23 LIFE …

# Life

Life isn't complicated, people are. No one is aware of their identity; bias; prejudice; ambitions and goals, when they are born. In fact, we aren't even aware, who our parents are, we are all born as strangers to strangers ( our parents ) . And, it's while living our lives that, we learn to create our own complications, whatever they might be. We are born free, without any burden, but as we live, we somehow learn to convince ourselves that, our self created burdens are what life is, or should be, but is it ?

# 24 WHY WE DO, WHAT WE DO...

# Why do we do, what we do ?

While having dinner, the mind that is me was exploring a thought. And here is the end product of that thought, please do share your views on it. Will appreciate it. So I was wondering, is there a way of knowing that, somehow we are or maybe, getting a guidance from the Universe without releasing it? Sounds quite stupid and unscientific, isn't it, but is it ? The question I asked myself is, why do we humans do whatever we do. For example, we have created religions, societies under one nation states, and then within societies there are sub societies. So many different languages, and the list goes on. There are those of us who crave power and dominance.

Why do we do all this ? Is it in our nature ? And then my mind somehow wanted to find a similar reference in Nature here on Earth and the bigger Universe. To see, if there is a comparison. So what do we see ? Well! from what we know so far of our universe, the universe has unlimited diversity within it, starting with different galaxies, Stars and solar systems, pockets of space which are just empty, followed by galaxies packed with powerful objects like super massive black holes among others. Also within the universe, energy and gravity are in a constant struggle for dominance. And the overall picture of our Universe is quite chaotic. In a way, there is nothing harmonious about the Universe. Then let us look at, what the nature has built here on Earth, starting with powerful tall mountains and the list goes. And as I see it, our ancestors have tried to simply mimic or in other words imitate nature and the universe at large, Possibly without knowing. We build tall and mega buildings to show our strength and might. The societies and nation states that we have created for ourselves, are in a way a reflection or can be compared to different galaxies and star system in our Universe. We carry the tendency to awe others with whatever we feel is our strength. Also, we continue to carry forward, what the psychologists call the costly signal that, we picked up from our animal friends, to awe and win over our preferred sexual partners. By showing them our strengths, be it our wealth or intelligence etc. So in all, aren't we just mimicking or playing out, what we see around us in the bigger Universe as well as nature here on Earth. We are carrying all these information without consciously realising it, but enacting then nevertheless. It's fun, isn't it ?

## Time for a BREAK ?

I wasn't too sure about the " morning musings ", but I thought, I will take the risk. Hope it was a good read. I will be quite interested in hearing your thoughts one day. Please do jot down your thoughts on the empty page.  To continue reading, please turn to the next page.

And in the next section, I thought, I will share my thoughts over coffee.

Thank you ....

( This page is left empty for your notes )

25 Thoughts Over Coffee:

## Failure

The stories of your failures will only sell, if people are convinced that, you eventually did succeed in the end

## You

This World is Special only because, YOU are a part of it

## Conflicts and Enemies

Our conflicts are of our own creation, and so is our society. What we solve are generally the unresolved ,and the unresolved are what creates our conflicts. We are all born free, and that is what we should all BE

## Your History

History is at the mercy of its authors, so don't let anyone else define you, in their own version of YOUR history. The " future of history " depends on who gets to write it, and that's how it has always been

## Humanity

An ONION is in its layers, and so is HUMANITY

## The Mind

We carry our values, cultures and traditions in our minds and they get reflected through and by our actions, and we judge not a person, but our own interpretation their actions or inactions

## Change and heroes

Change is an inevitable PROCESS and the only constant, and so is EVOLUTION. Circumstances make, break and reveal a MAN, and those who stand tall through the grinding PROCESS leave behind a lasting LEGACY as heroes, but HEROES aren't born they are ordinary folks made into heroes by their circumstances.

## God & Science

Through science, you can see all the evidence and also learn to describe, the beautiful and majestic work of a possible God. To know, what a God is or might be, you may need science and not just religion

## Man in the mirror

The man in the mirror is not you, but a reflection. And how you see, perceive and interpret that reflection is, completely dependent on the man you have learnt to be inside your own mind.

## Religion and peace

PEACE has no RELIGION, and being at peace with yourself and the world around you is all about the state of your own mind, and not the state of your religion

26 POEMS...

27 THE BIG SHOW ...

# The Big Show ..

I may have been playing a role
In a movie , now I know
The day I was born is
When  it all started to roll

I had no say
In starting the play
But I was enlisted anyway

Many before me
Who also came to the show
I know, have now departed

All the characters who
I have come to know
Are also playing their roles
As best as they know

We are all in the play
Writing our own stories
And building up the characters
As we all go

But how will it all end
No one seems to know

The movie is hundreds of
Thousands years old
And in it, for some
There is always glory and gold

Each of the character in itself
Is part of a story
That may at times feel
As a repeat of old

The Continuity of the show
Comes from the characters and their roles
Rolling on the stories
And that is how it goes

I hope the show goes on
And it continues to move on

There are many like me
In the show
Who will one day, have to go

Characters and the roles
People play, Come and go
And that is the
Design of the big show

# 28 THE STORY OF LIVE AND LIVING ...

The story of Life and Living....

I made a deal with life
And the deal was

As long as life
Is living through me
I will not get in the way
Somehow I knew
I may not have much sway

No matter what
The process of living
Throws at me
I will chose life
And that's how
I have learnt to Survive

Finding a way
To navigate away

It is living that
Makes a life interesting

Powered by life
Living is not just
About learning to survive

Life can only be experienced by living
This is the story of
Life and living

Next page...

# 29 A FRIEND ...

## A friend...

Friends I made
Are not to be short changed
I hope to be with them
Until the end of my days

That is what I say
To myself now almost everyday

The memories of me
That I have
Has people and places in it

People who I have met
The places I have seen
And sometimes the experience
Has also been quite mean

Strange are humans
Or so I feel
We tend to chase
And struggle with
The outcome we can't take

What logic says is logical
Yet it is hope
That help us
Win the day

Sad is not what I feel
Lost is probably, what I am

When a good friend
I thought I had
Has somehow gone bad

The road ahead is quite long
And it is the friends
That you will need
Sometimes, just to carry on

Whisper or scream, all you may
To let out all
Your hurt and pain
But it may be in disdain
If a friend is not there
To help you see
Through the pain

# 30 YOUR HOME ...

Your home...

Alone is how
I was born
And alone is
How I will end

I fear, it's a story
My fellow humans
May end up writing
Again and again

Living may make them hallow
A feeling that
You would say
Is quite hard to swallow

Waiting for rescue
When it may not be coming
Hoping in despair
Yes I know
You may say
Now that's not fair

Carrying the burden
In a way
That you feel the pain
Pouring down as rain

The sorrows won't
Get washed away
But try all you may

Treacherous winter is underway
You crave for summer

To come your way

You are being sent
To the gallows
It is how you may feel
And shelter from
All of it is
What you want and need

Your home is in you
And you are your shelter
When you learn to realise this
Then you may not falter

# 31 CHANGE...

# CHANGE ...

Powerless is how you feel
When you have no control
On the direction of your sail

And your own circumstances
May make you feel
That you are about to derail

Control is what you think
You should have
That is what you want and wish for

You aim to control
The direction of winds
So you can sail on
As the way you wished

A constant struggle is
What you feel
Living your life is no joke
That's how you think it is

You had no say
In your own creation
Genes that make you
Are also borrowed

Where and how
You were born
Was a choice
But not your own

So why is it
That you always
Want to be in control

Maybe it's your human nature
Or you think that's how
You were born

It maybe true somewhat
Feeling you are special
Is true for you
But not a fact

You happened without your say
Your journey will end
On that you also
You will have no say

Powerless you were always
That's the big picture
Which you fail to see

Living is what you can do
Life isn't going
To listen to you

Try you may
All you want

A perception of control
Is probably want you want

No ! don't surrender
It is not
What I say

The situation you are under
Will not have a final say
A change is always underway

Change is what
Will change things
As Power is powerless over change

# 32 YOUR VIEW..

Your view....


The war you are fighting
Is within you, I say
And so is your world
Where you now stay

Your past and your future
Is being written
In the present

What you loved
And what you lost
May not be
The end after all

Your world matters
To you, you say
But it is only because
You let it matter
Won't you say

In the beginning
When you didn't exist
Nothing existed for you
And this is the truth


Your identity and who you are
Is what you have
Learnt to be

Protecting your pride
Along with your tribe
Is probably what makes you thrive

You get hurt by words
And others get hurt
From your actions and reactions
Is this not the curse
Or the world
You are struggling
To live with

Call me, when you need me
But call me also
When you don't

Let us talk
And let us talk more
Tell me, why you hurt so easy
And just why do words
Make you so dizzy

People don't understand you
This is how you feel

Sometimes those who
You like or love
May love you also
But not as
You may want them to

Who and what
You are to someone
Depends on how they see you

Your perspective is
Just your point of view
And your views
Will also reflect you

What your world
Is to you will always
Depends on you

When it rains
You may look for a rainbow
But the rain is not
What bothers you
How you see the rain
Will always have a hold on you

A change in you and how
You understand the world
Will bring about
The change in your view

33 TO LIVE AND LOVE AS DIVINE..

# To live and love as divine...

Ready to love
I felt I was
But a love
I knew nothing about

Little did I know
About human emotions
And how sticky
It could be

Clarity that you seek
Will come wrapped
In weeps of complexity
Digging deep disturbing your sleep

You took a turn
And may be it was
A wrong one

But turning around from it
Is much easier said than done

The road will be slippery
You may slip and fall
Tears will flow
Down the hall

Humans are complicated
That I have realised
And loving a human
As would say is
Most certainly not advised

And that was also
My thought process
For a while

Until the day
When a thought opened
My mind to the possibility

That maybe the love
We seek is because
Somehow we feel incomplete

Complete is how
We are born
Incomplete is what
We make ourselves feel

Issues that matters
Are all in our minds

It is when
We are fine
In our minds
That we learn
To live and love as  divine

## 34 MEMORY OF YOU..

## Memory of you....

A ghost is not
What she was chasing
But a memory of you
She thought, she would keep

Moments of magic
That made her feel
It will last forever
Or at least until
She is unable to breath

The joy you were
To her, it seems
Is what you felt
Was nothing but a routine

Where do you go from here
Answers to which
May never be clear

Why and how
Will make you ponder
Weighing heavy on your
Heart, mind and shoulder

Memory of you
Is all what is left
Frozen in time
Until she learns to forget

35 MINE...

# Mine....

I owned nothing
And I owed nothing
Sitting here is
What I ponder

Greatness is what
Some like to pursue
That is true

To lead is their calling
It is what they believe in
And intend to do

Give the world a direction
To pursue a journey and prosper

Shine the light
So others can
Live and be nurtured

The moments of magic
Is a pursuit
That some as leaders
Strive to do

All that seems fine
But I will prefer
The aged wine

Sit with me in tranquility
A place inside my head
Where there is no hostility

It Couldn't careless
Is how it feels

I sense the need to change
But the change should in me

Make myself better is
What now I intend to seek

Nothing will matter
When I will say
My farewell to thee

The glory and greatness
Will all be left behind
As I learn to understand life
I know, nothing  I thought
I was and had
Was ever truly mine

# 36 REDEMPTION...

# Redemption ...

She said loving you
Is my redemption

The story of me
Is also a story of you

It has, I and you
That is your clue

I couldn't resist to say hello
So hello is what I said

You made the magic happen
By saying, and hello to you

We connected from there on
As if we were never disconnected

I hope the magic carries on
Until the day
When there is no night or dawn

Together let's make memories
Where Part of me
Will be lost in part of you

You will be my addiction
And as crazy
As it may seem
That is how I feel, she said
I will be redeemed

## Time for a BREAK ?


Hope you enjoyed the ten poems. I wrote them as random thoughts, at least that's what I thought while writing, but they were probably not random at all. And I wonder if you were able to relate to them? If you did then, please do jot down your thoughts on the empty page.  To continue reading, please turn to the next page.

Again, we are taking a break from poetry in the next section, and then we will go back to it. Let's take it as an experiment, shall we ? Hopefully you will like it, and if it's a bit too much then, please do accept my sincere apologies.


Thank you ....

This page is for your notes

( I have left this page empty, because it's only on an empty page that you can write something magical and beautiful. So if you want to write something or note down a thought that pops into your mind then, please do )

Next page ...

# 37 IMAGINATION@WORK..

# 38 BEING ANCHORED BY OUR OWN MAKE-BELIEF

# Being anchored by our own make-believe

I find myself in a place that looks and feels like Mumbai in India, but much cleaner, and there is something about this Mumbai that feels quite different. So I am trying to absorb the new Mumbai through my senses. The hustle and the bustle still feels of the Mumbai that I know it to be, but I keep feeling that, there is something different about this city.

So While running around as a tourist, I decide to stop a cab, and ask the cabby, to take me to a place where he would like to go personally. We drove for a while, and then he stopped at a place, which looked to me like an open public park. I got out, and decided to take a walk with him.

And while walking along, I see all types of statues suspended in the air, some posters left on the ground, and people speaking to themselves. Some are crying their hearts out, and some are just frustratingly angry. There are also those, who seems to be asking for their problems to be solved. But they are all speaking to themselves, and not to each other. I stood there for a while just trying to understand, where I am, and what is this all about. I see the cabby gentlemen glued to observing a woman dressed in purple. She seems to be crying her heart out while speaking to herself about many of her issues. So I asked the gentleman, do you know her, and he said yes. She is to me, what my grandmother was to my grandfather, my wife. I said interesting, so why don't you go give her a hug, it seems to me that, she needs it. And he said, I am

113

seeing her in the evening, and that's when I will give her a hug, but we won't be discussing anything.

For now, I just want her to see me standing here at a close distance, and be aware of the fact that, I am here with her. You see, all these people do know each other. The old guy, who on his knees crying, he is the head of the city government. And you can tell that, he is struggling to cope, he is also like us, a human being. We come here to this place, to speak to ourselves openly, and everything we say here remains here, as some educated people will say, highly confidential. It will not get discussed outside. That's how it works here, and we will all go back to our daily lives. It was a very different experience, but a very good one. I thought, why not, let me give it a go. So I decided to unburden myself of all the things that, I was carrying inside my mind. And when I was done, I realised, it's evening already. I go out of the park, and decided to catch a train from the nearest station.

And there I was sitting in the train, which looks more like a regular commuter train , but no body is standing. While departing from the station,I hear an announcement, and it's about people who have gone missing, and also about the passengers, who bought the tickets but aren't travelling, for whatever reason. The announcement is about wishing them all well, and asking people to look after each other. I couldn't help but smile. What an interesting train ride, I said to myself.

But then after a while, the train started to slow down, so I went up to see what's happening. And there, I see what looks like hundreds of people walking on the rail track, some were even walking in front of the train. I can see a

young girl dressed in a blue top and a denim short,
walking recklessly in front of the train.

So I asked the driver, what's going on, don't these people
know it's dangerous, and they will die ? And he said, yes
sir ! That's what they are here to do, they are here to try to
die. This 2 km line is known as suicide zone, and that's
why now we don't run driverless train on this line. But
don't worry sir!, give them 5 minutes. And he was right,
the track started clearing up after 5 minutes. I was
shocked and quite confused. Therefore, I asked him if, he
would help me understand what was that all about it. He
said, sure sir! I will now put the train on self drive mode,
and then we will talk. He comes out of his cabin, and
said Sir! Did you notice the young girl dressed in a blue
top and a denim short ? I said Yes! Well, she is my
daughter, and until today, I had no idea that she wants
to kill herself. I said, oh Gosh! I am so sorry. And he
responded by saying, no sir! I am happy to realise that, I
have to be a better father to my kids. So I am glad, I saw
her on the  track today. People get overwhelmed, and life
gets difficult for all of us at times, but when some of us
decide to try to kill ourselves, by coming to the suicide
zone, they realise that, it's not just them, but hundreds
and thousands of people like them are feeling the same.
They get talking which each other, and also their friends.
And somehow without fail, they decide not to kill
themselves. Seeing my daughter here, I have realised, I
have to be a better father, and if you allow me, let me call
her, and tell her I am sorry.

I got off the train at the next stop, and kept walking. I was
letting all what I experienced sink in, but I had a smile on
my face, so I kept walking. And then I bumped into a
lady, who use to be one of my best friend while we were

studying in the university. I looked at her and said, bloody hell! You died so many years ago, and just what are you doing in this city, if I remember correctly, you have never been to India right ? . But never mind all that, so good to see you bud! She smiled and then burst out laughing, and said " I know what you are thinking buddy, remember I know your mind, and no, you are not in any parallel universe ". I laughed with her and said ok, you got me, so where the hell I am ?. And she said come here, sit with me, and I will show you.

So I sit there with her, and see someone who looks like me, sleeping on the same bed where I would normally sleep. And she said " bud! this is your dream, and in that dream, this is all your imagination ". And I said to her, aah! I got it .

We don't really control our dreams, or thoughts. Yet they get created inside our minds. We want to be in control of lives, but we can't even control, how we feel and what to feel. The idea of being in control is my own make - belief. Is it not ?

I keep all my precious things in my imagination, because I have realised, there I can never lose them. Mind is a tool, and I am learning to use it better everyday. I know, just like me, many of my fellow humans struggle at times, and go through the normal process of living a human life. Sometimes, we don't have answers to many of our questions, and living a human life can be quite overwhelming at times.

The idea that someone is out there, is a remedy in itself. We can't always help everyone, but if I can make their lives better by sharing the story of my own living as a

reference then, why not ? We believe in what we need to believe in, just to carry on. And even when we don't believe, we still have to believe that, we don't.
Some of us are convinced that a GOD maybe watching over them, while others simply carry a belief that, no matter what, eventually things do get better.

I look at the stars and the universe, and somehow feel that, I maybe able to converse with them, albeit in my mind. I have no proof or anyway of finding out that, I can in fact converse with a Universe. Also how do I know that the universe understand a human language ? I don't know the language of the Universe, and no one does for that matter. Yet I continue to converse with a Universe, a universe that probably doesn't know or care that humans refer to it as a Universe.

The idea that a Universe will bother to hear me out, in a language that humans created, and not only understand me, but also bend over for me to deliver my wishes is, probably nothing but a make - belief. And I probably know that, but nevertheless, it feels good, and it keeps me anchored. Without being anchored by someone or something, it will be very difficult for a human being to live a life.

# 39 IN AN IMAGINARY CONVERSATION WITH TWO ALIENS ….

# In an imaginary conversation with two Aliens

So I bumped into two aliens, who were supposedly on Earth on a reconnaissance mission. We didn't know each other's language, and that made communication a bit difficult. But being the curious person that I am, I somehow managed to convey a message asking them to plug into my brain, so we could communicate better. We got all connected and wired up to the same network, and the exchange of thoughts began. We were all able to read each other's thought.

During that exchange, I realised that they have been watching a lot of alien invasion movies, and some of them were quite old really cause the graphics were pretty primitive. So obviously, I decided to interrupt the proceedings, and asked guys through my thoughts, " do you realise that the movies you have been watching are decades old, and you have probably just managed to pick up those transmission signals that were lost in space some 30 plus years ago ".

But then, I discovered that these aliens were in fact lost, and have been around on earth for too long. And this got me really excited. I felt like a mega lottery ticket winner without really buying one, but never mind that, so not wanting to lose the opportunity, I thought, I'll ask them some questions, which I obviously did, and in the process discovered that their favourite human beings among our ancestors were people, who we tend to refer to as God like or saints.

And during the exchange, I further realised that the aliens were of the view that, all these individuals were born like any other human being, but went on to become extraordinary individuals, and their good acts and amazing individual journeys, focused solely on improving humanity. And their acts somehow later got classified as God like, by those who followed them.

Overtime humans started to worship some of them as the messenger of Gods, but in doing so, the real message that some of these individuals originally carried and whatever they stood for, got lost into books written by those ,who decided to write and describe these individuals and their amazing individual journeys in their own version. And these books along with the literatures later became the gospel and part of religious texts. Today some of these individuals are brand names, and have religions are built around them. Also what the aliens found quite amusing was, how we as humans created a fictional character like the " Santa Claus " and made him into over a trillion dollar worth brand.

Anyways moving on, so while I was quite intrigued by their thought process, I couldn't help but go back to all the alien invasion movies that I have seen so far, so with that in mind, I asked them" Guys are you seriously going to invade Earth one day " ? On that they laughed and laughed, and then said, are you serious ( very much in a movie like manner ) ? My response was, of course, I am! And their response was. First " earth " is not the property of Human Race, you as a  human  in the current shape and form can't survive in an extreme weather condition anywhere else in the universe, so your kind need to be thankful to the same Earth you claim to own. You are fragile and your death is written the very day you are born, but most of you are obsessed with the concept of ownership. And second, if you go back in Human history, it is your kind that has been quite busy invading each other for whatever reason your species could come up with. And with regards to GOD, what makes you think that only humans have ownership over a GOD ? . You created a concept, and you want to own it, that's understandable.

But answer me this, if you can. Do you see your kind invading the ANTS ? Is there a reason for humans to eliminate ants as a species ? The estimated population of ants on earth as estimated by humans is roughly around ten thousand trillions, yet there seems to be no existential clash between the two species. In fact humans aren't at war with any other spices apart from their own. Your kind annihilate each other through weapons designed to kill your own kind.

So yes, I can see how your fear of an advance and evolved alien race invading humans, could make sense to you. But to us, your kind is equivalent to what you call an ant. And may be that answers your question .

# 40 WHEN I MET AN IMAGINARY FELLOW HUMAN BEING FROM THE DISTANT FUTURE ....

# WHEN I MET AN IMAGINARY FELLOW HUMAN BEING FROM THE DISTANT FUTURE

As a human being, I've a lot to apologies for. And let me begin with my sincere apologies to my fellow human beings, who were persecuted, thrown into death camps by a group of human beings, for being considered different. I also have to apologies to hundreds of thousands of those, who had to lose their lives because of a decision taken by another group of humans, to drop one of the most deadliest weapons created by humans to annihilate their own kind, in order to end, and win a war. I have to also apologies to thousands, who continue to lose their lives, because we fail to look past our differences.

None of us are born with our enemies. Our enemies are of our own creation. I apologies to humanity for not being able to influence the past, and for not having the ability to stop the atrocities committed by a group of humans on another, just to further their self interest; bias; ideology, and what not.

Yes, I am a human of extremely limited abilities, but as a human being, I would like to commit to you HUMANITY that, I'll do my small part, whatever that might be. I submit to you HUMANITY that, my rights, privileges, and freedom will not come at the cost of infringing other's rights, privileges and freedom. My opinion, ideology, beliefs shall not supersede or suppress others. I am not here to rule, but to experience. I submit to you Humanity that, as a human being, I shall learn to forgive the past, and make my own contribution in shaping a better world for all, where the next generation of HUMANS are born free, free of any historical baggage, free to create and invent or reinvent their own destiny.

I know, and I believe that the real potential of Humanity is limitless. And a world in which a human being will stand by a fellow human being, will, in my opinion be the Kingdom of heaven that some of us chase. I know that, we create our own hell and heaven.

In my imagination, I met a fellow human being from the distant future, he showed me the various possible outcome of Humanity and the future of Humanity. And told me, all this is subject to the decisions humans will make today, as our future is a feedback of our present. I woke up, and realised that I may have been dreaming, but I can still remember him say, don't let me down, don't think that you won't be heard, and don't ever doubt that, I am

because you are , and because of you, I WILL Be.

# 41 A DREAM, AND THE " I " IN ME....

# A dream, and the " I " in me

So I find myself in a medical lab, and there is this lady wearing a synthetic white suit working hard, carrying out test procedures on patients. And I can see that, she going through the list, and calls the gentleman, whose turn it is, to get tested. Following the procedure, she puts him in a suit bag, pumps air in it, and then slides him inside a scanner. He gets claustrophobic and starts panicking, and in doing so starts having a go at the lady. He is screaming and asking her to increase the air supply, which the lady says is against the guidelines, and may also compromise the test results. I sensed that he was clearly in no mood to listen to her, so he starts to tell her that, her JOB is to serve him and people like him, by following their orders. The lady looked quite distressed, so for whatever reason, I found myself telling the lady to do whatever the gentlemen is asking for, and then let it go, as its not worth the effort. And she did exactly that, but after the test , the gentlemen carried on with the abuse and also threatened to take actions. I heard all that, and then asked the lady to ignore all that, and not bother herself.

That complex and stressed situation somehow came to an end, and it was getting late, so she decided to close down the facility and leave. And there, I saw a nice young man waiting for the young lady just outside the glass door. After closing the facility, we both come out together, and I greet the young man, asking him to take care of the young lady, because she had a rough day at work. Hearing that, he invites her for a coffee, but the lady looked quite SAD. Which sort of made me ask her, if she was FINE, and she replied, sir, please look at the note in your right pocket, and then she went away. In the note, she wrote, " this young man likes me and I like him a lot also, he gives me hope, but he doesn't know that I am a HYBRID HUMAN, and you know the Organics ( Human ) attitude towards us ". After reading the note, I felt a bit sad for her, but kept walking anyways, as it was getting quite dark. And on my way, I bump into someone I felt looked quite familiar. He and his colleagues were out with a group of kids in the snow. The kids were all wearing identical red school uniform , and seem to be having fun playing outside. Looking at all that, I couldn't help myself, so out of curiosity, I asked my friend, why is your school open at night ? And he said, well, you know, ORGANICS ( HUMAN) don't want their kids to study with HYBRIDS so we have to find a way around it. I shook my head in dismay and decide to carry on walking. And then, I came across a group of young adults who sounded quite annoyed, and I could hear them complain about how the HYBRIDS are now taking over their resources, so they have to stop all them before it's too late. Then I also heard them talk about blowing up a building that was housed by the HYBRIDS, so I decided to intervene, and asked them to think again. And while we were discussing, a young kid took out his GUN, and decided to shoot me. And while being shot, I asked them, why did they shoot me, when we were simply having a chat, but they ran away. I fell on the ground, and I felt that, my fall pressed a gadget that I was wearing. In almost no time, I see a group of futuristic looking paramedics type people surrounding me, and asking me, if they could help me. I blinked as a sign that I thought meant YES, so they started treating me.

They plugged my body in the equipments that they were carrying, and told me, it is to stabilise me and lower the pain. And then, I heard them say that the nearest hospital to treat my wounds is a bit far, but they will try to get there on time while assessing my condition. And in the transporting vehicle that they were carrying me in, I saw a familiar face. It was the same young lady from the LAB. But before I could say anything , she and her friend asked me, why did the ORGANICS shoot you ? Didn't they know that you are also an ORGANIC ? I smiled, and said, let me share with you a story. Long before you guys existed, we the ORGANICS were quite good at killing each other. Do you see these buildings around you ? They replied YES, and then said " as we understand from our literatures, these beautiful architecture were developed and built by ancients ORGANICS". And I said yes, they were different places of worships of the ancients. The one where I was shot was called a CHURCH, and other one here was once known as a Buddhist monastery, the other two are mosque and a temple.

During my time, we the ORGANICS use to come to our different places of worship, to worship our GODS. And there were many incidents, where we the ORGANICS killed each other in the name of our GODS. Also, we the ORGANICS use to persecute other ORGANICS for being of different culture, race, tribe among other things . So throughout our history, the ORGANICS have killed each other. And in a way, me being shot by another ORGANIC confirms the fact that we haven't changed much. The paramedics smiled, and then asked me, please tell us, " are our GODS also your GODS " ? So in response, I asked them, tell me about your GODS. Then they showed me the pictures of their Gods. After looking at the pictures, I smiled and said, the bald gentlemen with glasses was known as GANDHI in his time, the lady wearing the cotton clothing was known as MOTHER Teresa, and the other two gentlemen are Mr Mandela and Martin Luther King. In fact, Mr Mandela died during my time, and many world leaders at the time attended his funeral . So no they are not GODS, but ordinary ORGANICS who became extraordinary through their own journey, and all of them championed the cause of the persecuted and always fought for others right. And do continue to look up to them for inspiration. But I believe, they would have told you themselves, to never worship them as Gods. And while I was talking, I hear an alarm go off. The paramedics started looking a bit anxious, and one of them asked me, if I would opt to have a mechanical heart transplant done, because my ORGANIC heart is giving up and they couldn't find an ORGANIC heart in their database that is available immediately, and also that could work with or be accepted by my body. So I said no worries, change the destination and take me to an organic incubator, and there you will find a stored organic body that I could possibly use, and then, all you have to do is to use my unique code to match with the other body and transfer my mind into it. They found the incubator and the stored body, and started the process, but I could see a shade of disappointment in their eyes. So I told them please don't think that I am somehow being a hypocrite. I know, I can't fight for the cause of HYBRIDS being a HYBRID, so I have to work inside and with the system, in order to change it. Also,I don't intend to stop unless and until I see real progress. And while you are transferring my mind into the new body, do look at my historical memory, and there you will find that the place where we are today was once known as AFRICA. And when I use to come here, there were no snow on the streets at the time, it was the continent where many ORAGNICs believed, the process of HUMAN's evolution from their animal ancestors started.

We the ORGANICS can't survive the changing world or explore the UNIVERSE to find our answers, so it is up to you, the HYBRIDS to carry and take the HUMAN RACE forward, and this is why you all came into BEING. They all listened, and then asked, " do you or did you ever wondered like us the HYBRIDS, why you the ORGANICS exist and what is your purpose and this world you find yourself in " ? I smiled and said, you know, in fact, I remember quite clearly the night when I wrote a down note, and although, the thoughts at the time seemed like an acceptable answer to me. I did go to BED a bit disappointed, and in my attempt to find a better answer through my mind, I tried to reach out to the UNIVERSE as I would always do, to help me find my answers. So I asked the UNIVERSE that while I sleep , in my dreams or through my dreams please guide my thoughts and help me tap into a thought process that will help me develop a better answer for my questions on why I or the world exist. I think you will find that note in my memory somewhere, please do look for it . And there it was, so I asked to read the note, marked my thoughts today, and it read, When I was YOUNG, life and everything about LIFE looked and sounded as FUN. But it is not FUN that attracted ME to LIFE the most, there was something intriguing about LIFE itself. And as I grew older, LIFE started feeling heavier. While ageing, I realised that I've started carrying baggage, I wasn't born with. I've always wondered, what is this cycle of LIFE & DEATH, and just why do I have to be a part of it ? What is my purpose and role, and is there a purpose to the world I find myself in ? I am aware, I am a HUMAN, a human with extremely limited abilities and capabilities. So while asking questions for which I had no answers, I found myself on a journey, only to realise that I may never find a perfect answer. Why I or the world exist is, a question that many have asked before, and in their quest for answers they found themselves on a journey, which helped shape them into the person they became. And although they do not exist today, their individual journeys lives on, inspiring and guiding many. The " I " in me is still looking for answers, knowing very well that there may be different variation of acceptable answers to the questions, I've been asking, just like there could be many paths to a destination. Today, I know that the elements I'm made from came from a dying STAR that once existed. My existence was only made possible because of the DEAD star, so through me, in a way, the dead star continues to exist. In short, life finds a way to continue to go on, in a different shape or form. So life is basically an interconnected WEB, and it might very well be that I am just a tool through which LIFE found a way to carry on. The answers are many and so are possibilities, and as long as there is LIFE in me, I think the " i " in me will keep looking for answers while exploring the possibilities. They all read my note for me, and smiled, and then said, " may be this is a dream, and may be through your DREAM you find yourself in a distant future of HUMANITY. But the question is, did you find your answers " ? And while all this was going on, I heard a familiar sound, and it was getting louder and louder, only for me to realise that I was in fact in my own house sleeping on my bed, and it was time to get up.

42 BELIEVING IN SOMETHING....

# Believing in something

So I am in a place, that looks quite similar to a mall. We are running around, and then I decided to call it a day. I am told, we live on top of the mall, so I grab the nearest ladder, only to realise quickly that it is broken, but after a lot of trying, I managed to climb up to a platform, which is, I am told, the resident's floor.

I meet a lot of people there, and they tell me, how much, each of them paid for their residence etc. The most expensive one was as expensive as buying a big town. After our little chat, I was asked by someone, who I presumed knew me, to move to our quarter. We started walking, but somehow, I got a bit left behind, but then someone friendly offered me a ride. It was an open 4x4 type vehicle. We got on it, and it went through different places, some were extremely beautiful, but some weren't, and I remember asking the gentlemen, who was sitting beside me, about the tall tower, and I was told, it's where people come to learn cooking.

And then the vehicle ploughed into a very dry land with dry trees, and as we went through the dry forest, the ride got a bit rough, so I asked the driver, to go easy, but I was told, it's quite ok, and is nothing out of the ordinary. Then after a long ride, we got off the vehicle, and I remember being very thankful, because the ride was becoming very taxing on the mind and also physically exhausting.

We all got off the vehicle, and I was told my place is close, so I should keep walking, which I did. And after walking for a while, I found myself inside a metal building with unlimited floors. A friendly face walked towards me, and gave me the keys to open the door for an elderly lady, who was suppose to come up and meet us. I couldn't remember the appointment, but out of politeness, I decided to take the key, and attend to what needed to be done. And when I opened the door to the staircase, I found myself being overwhelmed by the number of stairs and floors, it seemed endless. So being overwhelmed by what I saw, I decided against it, and looked across to check for other available options. But all of the options looked almost identical, so I asked, if there is a lift? The friendly face looked at me with disappointment, and went to get the lady up on his own. And it took him less than a minute. Which did leave me quite perplexed. I remember asking him, how did you do that? And he said, well you could have done that as well, but you allowed yourself to be overwhelmed by the situation.

I was quite confused, so I asked the friendly gentlemen, if I could go home and rest, because I feel lost. And he responded immediately saying, you do seem lost today, you better go and get yourself sorted out.

Then someone offered, to take me home, I remember going through very dry land again, and it went on and on. But when I was getting more and more disappointed, the gentlemen said, ok that's your home. I looked across, and saw what looked like a very small green patch of land. I remember saying, Gosh! It's a very tiny place, but the gentlemen responded with an authoritative voice saying " just go inside ", and when I got inside it, I found it to be endless. I felt so comforting that, it made me feel at home. And while admiring the beauty of the place, I wondered, if I could only transport myself to a place like the Grand

Canyons, and to my surprise, there I was. I found myself in place that looked like the Grand Canyons. It was very peaceful, and I was wilfully lost, until a gush of wind reminded me of where I was.

There I saw a young man talking, and when I asked him, who he is talking to, he said, can't you see ? I am talking with my father, and he has a message for me. But I saw no one, just him. So I decided to leave him to whatever he was doing, and carried on walking, only to find a boy, who looked almost like me, with a device in his hand, reading a written post, which he said was thousands of years old. And the post was talking about " virtual reality merging with whatever is physical reality, and all that being operated by an advanced artificial intelligence ". I read through the post, and asked the boy " who are you ? And why are you reading this in the middle of no where ". He responded by saying, close your eyes and when your mind says, open them. Which I did, but only to find myself in a dark universe, it was too overwhelming. I couldn't think, but then a realisation started to sink in.

I started wondering, did I just experience by own life journey as a human ? The broken ladder was, my choice of convenience. I got on it, because it was easily available to me, only to regret it later. But somehow, I managed to climb up, and probably because of my relentless efforts and a belief of overcoming the challenges. The endless staircase was a human life itself that I found overwhelming, and therefore asked for a shortcut. And the small green patch was the opportunity that I wasn't able to grasp. And even when I was living a life of real comfort, in the little green patch which eventually became endless, I wasn't happy, so I imagined being in Grand Canyons.

The little boy was me, imagining the universe to be a merger of a virtual reality with whatever is physical reality, operated and managed by a complicated and highly advance intelligence. And the gentlemen talking with his invisible father was probably, how I see the idea of a messenger of God that we have conceived.

So in the end, it's our belief that keeps us going. Whatever that might be, and eventually, we tend to become what we believe. A human being crediting a God, or someone simply believing in the ability of things to work themselves out will, more or less have the same outcome. Some will claim that, it is their Gods that helped them, and some would say, it is their efforts and self belief. But in the end, it is all about " believing ". It is " Believing " that is, at the core of a human journey.

If you believe that a God is helping you then, you will learn to believe and feel that, it is probably the case, at least for you. But if on other hand, you believe that, there is no God then, that also requires you to believe that, there is no God, and you have managed to navigate your journey on your own. So therefore, you may say that, all you need is a self belief. With all this going inside my mind, I woke up, only to realise, I was late for a meeting, and while being on my way to the meeting, I thought, I will write this down.

# 43 NOTHING IS EVERYTHING - A MIND AT WORK....

# Nothing is everything - A mind at work

" A mind ", most likely has a mind of its own. And I am making this conclusion based on my journey so far. I am afraid the subject of psychology isn't really that developed, to help us see, a mind @ Work. A mind is an extremely beautiful thing. I would say, the most beautiful thing ever, but it depends on one's perspective. People want to be in control, but without realising that, they can't even control their thoughts or dreams. There are many theories around ,why do we dream and what's the purpose of dreams, but most of them are best guesses really.

Sometimes, you just don't know, why you do what you do, but you do it anyways. And that's why I am putting forward a theory " a mind has a mind of its own ". When you start to try to reverse engineer a mind, you slowly come to realise that, it's an amazing machine powered by beautiful algorithms. Our thoughts; ideas ; emotions etc are all powered by algorithm. Sometimes, we just don't know why, we come up with the ideas or thoughts that we do. It just comes to us. Clinical psychologists will need to expand their understanding of a brain.

Let's say there is a brain, which is mostly a hardware, but the mind is more of a self learning and ever evolving operating system. Which we use as a tool, to hate someone or build something remarkably beautiful. After putting my own brain and mind on trial for over many years now. I have realised that, I have really no idea why I do, whatever it is that I do sometimes. I have seen real virtual conflicts inside my own mind sometimes. So I work on training the mind, to learn to make good decisions especially right decisions. But then I realised, to make good decisions that are also right decisions, a mind needs to deploy a number of resources, and that's a process.

So before I ask my mind to make good decisions that are also right , I realised that, I need to give it the right tools. And these tools are, creating a very deep reservoir of wisdom; a strong situation awareness and judgment skills; ability to foresee things ; a skill to be able to accurately assess a situation ; a proactive imagination, and most importantly being able to let go. They are all important resources embedded in the overall decision making infrastructure within our minds. When a mind has the right resources at its disposal, it does work better. But sometimes the same mind finds a way to lose interest in everything including people, and this could create a phase where a person simply loses all interest in living. Now psychologists tend to define this phenomenon as clinical depression, but I am quite confident that going forward, the definition will have to be re-examined, because what I am learning helps me understand that, a mind sometimes isn't interested in what you ( the entity that you have learnt to become ) maybe interested in, so it's important to continuously feed it with something. And that's natural happiness for a mind. I have also realised that " your intelligence " is not your property, and most importantly, there is no you. Whatever or who I think I am. I have simply learnt to become it inside my mind. And that's how I have also realised that, a God can only be understood, appreciated and explained through science not religion.

A mind conceived religion to understand and explain God, but while some minds got stuck in the idea of religion to appreciate and understand a God, others moved on to create science. In fact, there is no conflict between science, humanity and whatever a God could be. So the bottom line for me is " nothing is everything and everything will eventually become nothing "

# 44 A HUMAN BRAIN....

# A Human Brain

One weekend morning, I woke up not feeling good. I guess once you reach a certain age, you can't really take your body for granted. And it's one of the reasons why I got into yoga and meditation etc. But never mind that. What I was going to say is, I started my day with a splitting headache. And while there are many underlying reasons that could trigger migraine or headache, the facts is, we are still learning about a human brain. So that got me thinking, what is a human brain ?

Well! for starters, a healthy human brain has around 100 billion neurones with 100 trillion neural connections , and each of these neurones fires around 200 times per second. On average, a human being  lives for around 3 billion seconds, so just imagine the total number of signals a human brain has to process over its life time ? No doubt, its an amazing machine, and like any other machine, sometimes it will misfire and also breakdown. And the headache was probably my brain telling me, something isn't right.

Our smart phones and tablets do breakdown on us, and after a while we replace them with an upgraded version. In a way, they are not designed to last a human lifetime, but thankfully that's not the case with our brain. So for discussion purposes, I will assume that, our brain might be a cleverly designed quantum computer. And unlike most computers , a human brain is somewhat unique to each of us, in a way tailor made. Having said that, it may not be as unique, as we might think it could possibly be. For example, people are able to come up with similar ideas or theories, albeit with some differences. Also they are able to relate to similar experiences. So its worth exploring that, in all, there maybe few different versions of quantum operating system that, we tend to call " a mind ". And what version of the quantum operating system we inherit, maybe down to genetics, but not limited to genes only. Also it's quite plausible that, we can also continue to upgrade our own minds, in other words, the operating system.

The mind has an inherent ability, to continue to learn, and in the process change the human, who has inherited it. But the question is, is there a command centre somewhere within that operating system that is somehow also a tiny bit independent of the entire operating system ? Also, is it possible that, this command centre within the operating system, makes us unique and somewhat different from each other, especially in terms of our thinking etc.

In my mind, I am willing to consider a possibility that, a human mind, the nature and the universe are all a very sophisticated self learning systems. And the inherent design of the operating system is such that, as the system evolves, it builds a command centre, in other words " the entity ". In case of a human being, this entity learns to become the identity of a person. It evolves further, and then learns to wish and desire. It conceives its own realities and the perception of a reality.

So the human brain is in a way is the most powerful supercomputer known to modern humans. A supercomputer on quantum level. And all of us get it for free. Also the cost of running it quite cheap. It consumes 7 times less power than an average laptop. Also the networking along with the overall hardware is simply amazing. For example, a cubic millimetre of human brain contains around 4 km of neuronal "wires".

The Brain is what makes us, who we are. And the choices we make is the input that goes into the algo designed to help a human navigate through their journey in life. Nature is the best technological process ever created. And the awesomeness of nature's ingenuity is reflected through a human brain. It is probably the very best self learning operating system that there is, an operating system that knows how to create within it, a command centre, in the other words, the entity. And this entity is, what we are, or what we become. Our identity is fluid because our brain is fluid, but sometimes, some of us do get stuck in our self created idea or narrative, be it our culture, nationality or anything else for that matter.

Just imagine a possible future, where you could create various copies of your brain, and install them on different people, including those you didn't quite like. They will all be you, but they may look different. Or you could install them on machines / human looking robots and send them to explore the Universe. And if you ever get a chance to meet them, do know this that. Most likely, the brains installed on the machines / robots will not remain an exact copy of your brain, because what your brain might have experienced through them, would have changed your brain.

And this brings me to a related topic. We can't really conclude that, we humans or other complex life form for that matter, didn't start out as part of a programming. And in the same way, we can't really conclusively tell, what is natural and what isn't? The reason being, whatever existed  before we came into being as human species, we tend to consider them as natural. So it's quite plausible that, some part of our universe or our own design, may have been created by highly advanced civilisation, who are no more, and over time the technological signature of their creation along with their signs of their own existence and their technological signatures got lost. And whatever they created or conceived, became part of what we have learnt to consider today as a natural or natural phenomenon. For example, if humans were to completely disappear from Earth then, in just over a million years, most of what was created by humans on Earth will also disappear, and become part of the nature, more or less. And it will be difficult for any other civilisation to conclude that, a species who called themselves " Humans" might have evolved to become the most dominant species on Earth. And who knows through our existence, all of us are, in some way adding to the grand design of whatever the universe is?

It's an amazing puzzle, and many of us will keep trying to imagine a plausible explanation, and thereby adding to the

pool of ideas, we are exploring. There is a possibility that, the universe is never going to be an end product, because it will continuously change, so therefore there is no destination. Whatever our reality is, it's only a perception of reality. The acknowledgment and awareness that, we exist within a vast universe is already a significant jump, and a marvel of how much a human brain has evolved over time. And for all we know, we may just be getting started on a long road ahead

But I hope, we don't end up wasting our time on enslaving ourselves with ideas of our own creation. Be it money; religion ; culture among others things. Most of us work quite hard on keeping our body fit, but I wonder, how many of us work equally hard on keeping their mental health in order? Like our smart phones, it also needs care. Can you imagine, a human without a brain? Well, in order to do that, you will need a brain, won't you?

# 45 COMMUNICATION AND LEARNING IN THE FUTURE....

# Communication and learning in the future

## Human Connection Gateway Interface ( HCGI )

Imagine in a not so distant future, humans develop the ability to create a worldwide network connection that connects almost every HUMAN with each other, and the entire collective aka the human society. But this is done with a strong built-in safeguards, whereby, every human connection will be based on an approval process, in other words a human consent.

And any or every human will have the ability to connect with another human, without the need of a mobile phone or another similar device / tool. Each individual connection will be unique and direct through the " human connect gateway ( HCG) interface. So, my mind will be able to call another mind, and communicate, be able to share ideas as well as thoughts freely.

The " HCG " interface could also be connected with the internet- the World Wide Web ( WWW), to enable a human mind to learn and also download information or the knowledge it may be seeking instantly. And a series of Quantum super computers will be connected to the " HCG " interface, to help a human mind process all that information and knowledge along with the complex data analysis, at quantum speed. Eventually the " HCG " could also be connected to various space satellites as well as spacecrafts and telescopes, to enable faster learning and discoveries.

Imagine being able to download all the knowledge that humans have on a child's mind, what will it do to the traditional way of learning ? Knowledge and information along with experience could be uploaded and also deleted upon request. We could also upload personalities and characters. And the question is, will this all be an evolutionary upgrade or a disaster ?

The uniqueness of humans is in our imperfections, and our ability to adapt. What will become of humans, we don't know. But a human without human emotions, may not be the human some of us would like to transform into. What would a human be, if you take away the heart breaks, moments of madness and despair , or the joy and smile ?

# 46 THE SHAPE OF THE UNIVERSE AND HUMANS ...

# The shape of the universe and humans - Parts of different reality

Here is an idea that I have been exploring. It came to me, when I saw a small group of insects crawl up on a banana. I could see that, the insects had no way of knowing the entire shape and parameters of the banana.

They were simply crawling on it. And then, I tried to imagine being one of the insects. Initially, it was quite hard, but slowly I started to see things from a different perspective. Although, I couldn't probably think as an insect, but let's for a second imagine that I did. So as an insect, I am doing what comes natural to me, which is to find food by figuring my way around. And even though, I have learnt to realise that, a banana is food, but my physical limitations sort of becomes a hindrance to help me see the entire banana, and also where precisely is that banana located. So while crawling along, the insect is basically moving along the direction and contours of the banana, but the shape of the banana could potentially give the insects an impression that, their movement is somehow making them go through ups and downs, and the two insects crawling on the banana from different sides, could also eventually end up meeting, and then possibly assume that their meeting was somehow destined or a divine intervention. When all they did was follow different paths, which started with them being far apart from each other, but their crawling along the contours of banana, ended up bringing them together.

Yes, one could argue, why did their journey intersect, and was the intersection designed or planned, or simply a matter choice. In other words an outcome of a journey planned by the two.

The crawling of insects on different parts of the banana, may have felt somewhat different and unique to the insects. They may have felt that, they are going through a different phase in their journey, when all they were doing is, travel along the contours.

Now, let's replace the banana with the Universe and the insects with humans. We along with the Earth are moving along the space time, we have an idea of space, but we still haven't figured out the entire contour of Universe accurately. Our movement isn't really planned, even though we feel that it is. So we travel along the space, and in doing so find ourselves moving along the curves and bends of the Universe. And these curves and the bends, obviously seem and feel different, but they are how the Universe is shaped. The time that we feel as being different or passing differently is weaved in the shape of the Universe, and so is gravity. If we were stationary then, the passage of time will become or seem longer, and the changes will be less realisable. So quite possibly, we experience life differently, because we are moving through the Universe.

A human living on one side of earth will experience life differently to a human living high up on the mountains or somewhere else for that matter. And evolution also factors in the location. So is it possible that, gravity, time, and with time, past, present as well as future. All come about as different parts of a reality, because of the shape of the Universe ?

# 47 AN ATTEMPT TO UNDERSTAND LIFE, NATURE, UNIVERSE AND OUR CURIOSITY...

# An attempt to understand Life, Nature, Universe and our curiosity

So energy powers life and everything around us, but life is not energy. Then what could a life potentially be? Possibly, an emergent phenomenon that comes into being, because of various underlying factors conducive to the existence of life at play making life happen?. And once it's triggered then, there are different levels or forms at which a life can carry on existing. Be it in a simple life form as bacterial cell for example , or as a complicated life form that is a human being. And the recent development in science, where humans have  learnt to make synthetic life known as " Syn3.0 - minimal synthetic bacterial cell", with absolutely minimum genetic information, to grow or reproduce, sort of adds merit to the thought process.

" Prions " are considered lifeless with no genetic material, in other words, they don't have a DNA. Yet they evolve like any living organism with DNA, and can cause deadly brain disease in both humans as well as animals. We may also start to discover  life in our universe that have different DNA and building blocks of life than, living organisms here  on Earth. So in a way, maybe, there is nothing holy about " Life " , it's just a naturally occurring phenomenon.

Life can exist and live for longer in humans than in comparison to simpler life forms. And nature has created a vast range of hosts with the ability to house life. One way to look at all this might be, to consider a possibility that, nature is perhaps utilising life as a core ingredient or technology, to carry out its evolutionary engineering.

Nature has built an extremely diversified ecosystem of living species using a core technology that we call " Life ". We have learnt to live with the idea that, nature knows best. That is  maybe because, it is nature that has created and designed the entire system. And won't it be amazing to imagine a possibility where, what nature created would one day learn to develop the ability to create nature itself? Nature has fantastically used " life " as a core technology to build and create an awe-inspiring system. Information powered by chemistry to create physics and whatever is a physical reality. And then through a process of trial & error, creating laws that governs the entire system, to keep it all sustainable.

So what is nature then? Is it an advanced self learning supremely intelligent system that designs, creates and also operates the entire ecosystem?  Can it also be an offshoot of a superior system that is known to us as " Universe ". Or another way of describing it will be as part of a much superior system that is the Universe. The entire system works on regeneration, and nature has built a clever system that keeps creating and recreating. This is possibly why nature will keep finding ways to recreate itself. Nature as we know it on Earth is probably different to what it is on other systems across the Universe.

The knowledge that we have and what we know, we didn't create them, all of them already existed. We just found a way to learn them. All of what we need to know and much more is probably out there, and in a way inside of us. Because we are all part and parcel of what is the system i.e. the Universe. It all depends on our curiosity to know and learn. So our attempt to understand who we are will also help us understand nature and vice versa. And to do that is probably hard wired in our nature by NATURE?

## Time for a BREAK ?

Hi again! So how was Imagination@Work, I wonder if it was a good read? In my own view Imagination is more powerful than knowledge, and without imagination, we couldn't have conceived the modern day society. I have left an empty page for your thoughts, and please do jot down your thoughts on the empty page.  To continue reading, please turn to the next page.

And we are going back to Poems. Hopefully you will like it.


Thank you ....

Next page....

48 POEMS...

# 49 ENTREPRENEUR...

## Entrepreneur...

The story of an entrepreneur
Is what I would like to narrate
It has hardship and struggles
And also a lot of heartaches

Some come through
But some don't

And sometimes it's hard
To just get out of the gate
Opportunities may come
But it might be late

Going through ups and downs
Not knowing if all you have
Will one day come crumbling down

It's not easy
Being an entrepreneur
Let me just say

You may wake up with high hopes
But in the nights
You may feel low
And there are times
When your life
May seem moving very slow

That's the trajectory
And that's how it goes

Tried hard, but failed
And fail is
What you may know
Sometimes you may have
Nothing else to show

It's a bitter feeling
That you already know
But No! hold on
Don't let that bitterness grow

Dream you must
Of what's to come
And your hope
You know is
Your best friend

You with you
Stumbling along the way you go
Hustling is what
You have learnt to know

Circumstances will change
As change they say is
The only guarantee

When you chase profits
You may have a loss
Everything that you think
You may have
May even go for a toss

You will win some
And sometimes you will lose
This is the story

And it is what you choose

Respect is what
I have for you
My wish is that
You always grow

Be tender and be kind
To yourself and also those
Who choose to shine
As entrepreneurs of the modern times

# 50 IT'S OK...

## It's Ok ....

It's ok to be not ok
And it's ok to be lost

It's ok to hate the world
And have a raging heart

Don't let them tell you
Who you should be

It's ok to feel
You are not ok
And have no answers
To how long it will all last

Questions you ask
May come with no good answers
And all you can see is
Clouds and the dark

It's ok if the world ends
Nothing will forever last

it's ok to feel down and out
And not know
How to get out

No body knows
How life plays out

But live you must
For as long as you last

# 51 REGRETS...

Regrets...

Gone is the pain
The eyes can now
See through the rain

Time has made
The melodies timeless

Memories that were made
Are now frozen in time
And at times you may wonder
Is this a plan of
What they call a divine

The ocean has a floor
That is so deep
May be for all the secrets
It wants to keep

All journeys even when they
May seem endless
Do come to an end

And when you are lost
Learn to connect the dots
However difficult the plot
Live your life you must

Beautiful is all life
And so is death
Try to live it
With  no regrets

52 COLD...

Cold.....

When you feel that
There is nothing
To lose or gain

Your pain carries no secret
And you will not
Be the same

Let the wind carry you
To a place unknown
Where knowing is
No longer a burden
For you and your soul

Gravity has no meaning
And it will have no control

Free you are
From your baggage
And your goals

Heat will always flow
From hot to cold
Following that rule
What is dead
Will go cold

Live the life you are
To warm your soul
Before all what you are
Will turn cold

53 STARS...

## Stars...

The stars said
No you can't go
But yes we know
One day you will have to

And no It is not
The burden of pain
Or the sorrow of a loss
We know that will all pass

The joy it has been
To watch you grow

It is the death
Of one of us
That made you
As you know

A stardust you are
And always will be

Whatever you maybe
Going through , do remember
Your existence gave
Us all a purpose
So exist, we hope
You will want to

One day we know
You will have to go
And not because
That is your WILL

It is how
We were all designed
By whatever it is
That you know as divine

# 54 THE GAME IS YOU..

## The Game is you...

Sadness in your eyes
Reflects the state of your soul
Your heart is sore
And you can't take it anymore

You may want to run
As Living seems no fun

Wondering you are, as to
What have you done
To deserve all this burn
Or did someone do
That to you
And made you numb

Either way, you are chipping away
Feeling stuck in a horrible way

Break you will
If you carry the burden
You feel condemned
All of a sudden

The heat is strong
And you smell a defeat
Though you should know
The defeat is not imminent
But only if you
learn to use the heat
To feed what you may need

Bend your knees
But not to surrender

You need to bend
So you can mend
Navigating your way
To the sunny beach
Yes today may
Feel like a long reach
And you may say
It is easier for others to preach

You are only human
That you should know
And sometimes it's good
To let it all show

Fear not what you feel
It is how you will
Learn to heal

Be there for yourself
And build again, even if
Today you may have no say

The game is you
You should know
And Play you will have to
Because that's your show

Learn as you play
Move up on the way
It is always you

55 WHAT MADE YOU....

# What made you ...

Life is not a struggle, living is
It is living that makes you
Whoever you may have become

The world as you saw
When you were born
Has gone through a change

Moments as memories
May at times feel
As if they are
Flowing through your veins

Living is what all lives do
Whether it is a plant or you

Your story of living
Is also the story of you

When all is said and done
There will come a time
When you may not
Be able to run

Playing back the memories of
What was once you
You are looking at the world
With a changed view

At times the world
Probably got the best of you

The pain and the hurt
You felt, with no rescue
Somehow also made you

# 56 THE STORY OF ME....

# The story of me ..

What was mine once
Is now all left behind

I am dead, as you know
So now you are kind

I lived and found
Reasons to live for

Everything I had
I thought was all mine
And so was the hate
For my own kind

It was all about me
And how could it not be
As I could see, I was
The centre of gravity

I would always ask the divine
To grant me, all what I felt
Was rightfully mine

Living the life
On my own terms
And on it, my mind was firm

Peace and harmony
That I always sought was
Also to be on my terms

But life ran out on me
Leaving me in history

Now, there is no way to rewind
And I didn't get to meet the divine

The life I lived
Is now all lost to me
I see no light or sunshine

Nothing is what I am now
And as nothing is how
My own story began

That is the story of me
Whatever I thought, I once was
Is all now, just a history

# 57 GIVING LIFE A MEANING ...

# Giving life a meaning...

People who made me
Also raised me
I was a part of them
And always will be

They gave me a name
And also my identity
With them I have felt serenity

I was in such a rush
Couldn't wait to grow up
Leaving them behind
In a gush

The world awaits me
Or so I thought
So gone as
A wind I was

I saw a world
That was different to mine
And when I felt lost
I carried on
Through the dust

Who I was, I didn't know
Memories of my past
I had to let them go

Moving forward was
Part of the show

What am I
Doesn't matter anymore
Nor does the journey
To the shore

Tides are high
And sometimes low
That's how they
Tend to flow

Winds changed the direction
Of my sail
At times, I was left
Biting my nails

Sometimes the journey
Had no direction
With no time
For a resurrection

Into the gallows
I felt I was being sent
I couldn't borrow
Happiness on a rent

There was no
Time for reflection
So I carried on as
It said on the caption

Shadows of the past
Are now all left behind

As a faint signature of mine

Living may feel like a test
From it sometimes there is no rest

That is how it goes
It will keep you on your toes
Living they say, gives life a meaning
And there is no prescreening

# 58 CUSTOMER REVIEWS....

Customer reviews...


I thought I have died
And was on my to heaven
But little did I know
The heaven on the show
Was on the ~~77~~th floor

The lifts were out
Because of the budget cuts
So I was asked to climb up
Floor by floor

This is not
What I deserve
I said in my mind
Why are they being so unkind

I have been so good
That while living
I didn't even bother
A piece of wood

The fear of ending up in hell
Is how is I lived
And it is what drove me
To this idea of heaven that
Now seems like hell

Maybe I was mis-sold
An idea that was
Not as good as gold
But that is what I was told

I know, I should have done better
Not waited for the letter
And made my own view
After reading through all
The customer reviews

# Time for a BREAK ?

Hi there, if I may. I am quite curious to find out, how is the experiment of mixing poems with the morning musings, thoughts over coffee and imagination@work working out ? I took an intentional risk of conceiving the concept, with a view that, it is probably worth a try. And continuing with the experiment, the next chapters are a break from Poems. We are getting into Understanding Humans. Please do share your thoughts. I have left an empty page for it, so please do jot down your thoughts. To continue reading, please turn to the next page.

Hopefully you will like it.

Thank you ....

THIS PAGE IS FOR YOUR NOTES

# 59 UNDERSTANDING HUMANS...

# 60 THE PURSUIT...

# Understanding Humans- The Pursuit

Before humans came along, and the battle of sexes began, the first organisms living on earth over 2.5 billion years ago, who dared to engage in the act of sex were more like Adam and Evan than Adam and Eve. Sex was conceived by nature way before heterosexuality came into being, in other words, before males or females existed. The organisms at the time were mostly isogamous- which basically means something between male and female.

Even today organisms including of fungi, algae etc still practice isogamy. But over the years as nature mastered the process of experimenting with various life form that it could potentially create, it probably realised and quickly learnt that, the best way to create complex life form is, to create a reproduction model, where the organisms are able to reproduce a better and updated versions of themselves by mating with each other. And since then nature has cleverly conditioned male and female to mate, whether it's humans or animals. Also the attraction for physical appearance is smartly hard wired in the overall reproduction process, in order to make sure the offsprings are given a  strong chance of being a better version of the two specimens used to create them.

The system was sustainable because all life forms were part of each other's food chain, but somehow humans managed to escape that food chain. And now they basically control it also. But humans don't do just that, they also ponder, and that makes me wonder if, humans are trying to also emulate the process that created them aka the nature. They have created their own systems, be it religion; a nation state ; gods; culture ; economy and the list goes on. None of the systems or the ideas are perfect, and probably wont anytime soon, but that won't stop them from trying.

Humans have built machines, to build their machines, and most likely some day in a not so distant future, their machines will then learn to imagine and then make new types of machines.

The idea that nature ended up creating humans because it was simply experimenting makes sense. And it's most likely that, humans are a product of chance and probability. As humans evolve and develop over time, they are also learning to develop the ability to perfect the process that helped create them. Also as humans evolve, the gene editing technics like CRISPR developed by them, may some day enable humans to create better and upgraded versions of next generations of humans, without having to wait for nature to deliver the new editions of humans over millions of years through evolution.

So what drives humans to carry and move forward, without ever collectively getting overwhelmed by the burden of so many questions, and not knowing why it all began. Also is there a purpose ? And the answers to these questions to some extent also lies in the inherent design of how nature has conceived the life of a complex life form, be it a human or an animal. Nature has hardwired complex life form to have emotions along with other features and tools, to enable living. And it is the process of living that somehow also helps humans carry on without getting overwhelmed by the questions to which they are still searching for answers.

In the end, every life forms has an end, and that's how the process is designed, to keep the system sustainable and efficient. But while living, a human also learns to question, and find explanations. And for some, these questions can be quite overwhelming, taking them to a place that could be considered by some humans as sad and lonely. But they find a way, to pursue an explanation, in order to make a sense of things. And in that journey some find a divine force, and some simply die knowing that, they won't know everything there is to know, so they keep the flame burning and along with it the pursuit, by aspiring by others to carry on.

# 61 THE SOCIAL STRUCTURE ...

# Understanding Humans - The Social structure

Most modern organised human societies living on Earth is dealing with issues related to the society being construed along with the lines of people belonging to various categories. A category with smaller groups of people are classified as minority, and those with larger numbers are labelled as majority. And that has been the construct so far.

The construct which was originally designed to help the well-being of the society at large has, in fact ended up increasing the divide. Today the societies across the world are struggling with growing inequality, and this inequality is quite wide spread across the society. Which has led to rising social tension especially among those who feel that, they are being eroded everyday.

People are growing more resentful of each other especially if they feel that somehow, people belonging to other categories are gaining unfair advantage over them. That is more or less, a global trend today. And nobody seems to have an answer, but some are taking the easiest option, in the name of protecting and fighting for the rights of those, who they believe are being wronged. This is adding fuel to the fire that is burning the society from within.

So whats the answer, and is there a solution ? Well! It is not an easy subject especially because people are increasingly getting entrenched in their own views, and maybe, it's time for us to revisit the construct of the organised society. The idea of diving groups of people along the lines of minority and majority is quite discriminatory to start with. Any society over time will change, and that's quite natural. So trying to preserve the make up of a society however tempting will most likely create social tensions within the society.

In the current construct, a society has no formal agreement on what people's obligations are towards each other and the society at large. Also while most nation states have a constitution to help them govern. These concept framed as constitutions are quite a complex for average people to interpret or understand. Also there is no real emphasis on creating an universal citizens charter, a framework with set of rules designed to evolve over time. That could serve as a legal agreement between individuals and the society at large, spelling out the role of the society and individuals making up the society.

The governments could then create services incorporating the citizens charter agreement, whereby those failing to comply with the charter could be penalised. There will be no majority or minority commission, just a citizen's charter, a universal agreement between people and the society.

Conditioning the society in a minority and majority concept isn't working out. People are naturally inclined to create a sense of belonging, so even within groups of people belonging to a majority and minority population, there will always be subgrouping of some sort over time. For example, a nation state with only one group of people will eventually get divided into various sub groups, and there will be subdivisions, so the make up that society will change over time . And this is inline with how nature works. Children's from same parents grow up to be quite different from each other, they create their own unique bond with each other as well as their parents, and some simply disconnect for whatever reasons.

A universal citizens charter will allow people to have their unique relationship with each other as well as the society while maintaining a common bond, whatever that might be. But that bond won't be permanent, and therefore it will be need to continuously evolve over time. The idea of a nation state or a society has limits, so the societies more adaptable and willing to change, might survive longer together than others.

# 62 THE ONE TRUE GOD ...

# Understanding Humans- The One True God

"To you, let your GOD be, what you want or believe it to be ". The idea of one true GOD could work on a sustainable basis if, every human being was capable of believing in one and the same thing over their entire life time. And also a situation where every human being alive agrees to believe in the same thing, goes against the construct and uniqueness of a human mind.

The human mind isn't designed to work like that, so personalisation plays a KEY role. For example, we are learning to fight cancer by personalising the treatment, and seeing success. So not only mentally, but physiologically also, one solution may not apply or work for every human being. Therefore tailored solutions targeting different individuals is now becoming a norm, more or less. Learning is also being tailored to specific students.

Our minds are designed to interpret things differently , and thus, we tend to have a range of different views on a subject matter. And there is a strong reason, why nature designed, a human being, the way it did. If our immunity response to a VIRUS or disease was identical or same then, we may not have a humanity today. We also respond to a given situation differently. And this overall understanding of human beings, may have played, a key role in why some of the ancient civilisations were tempted to create an idea of personalised GODs.

If we understand the Greek mythology correctly then, we are talking about a dozen of Gods with different roles. Another idea, which is a collection of many different philosophy and cultural traditions. Created million of Gods, each with a specific role. And that thought process created literatures that gave birth to Vedas and important practical knowledge like YOGA among others. These literatures were somehow later given religious context, and then, parts of the literatures were used to support a specific religious view point. But in the process, the knowledge and original message probably got ignored.

In my personal capacity, after spending years trying to understand religion, I have come to a realisation that, the literatures that form or create the modern day Buddhism and Hinduism are, basically a compilation of teachings, aimed at helping human beings. Having said that, the religious connotation of these literatures, has been a great disservice to humanity.

The message that the so called messengers of GODs gave, for and behalf of their own version of a GOD was, never from a GOD, but their own. In a way, it was quite cleverly packaged. I do have great admiration for their work, but not for the religions that were later created by the followers of various religious ideology , based on their own interpretations of the messages.

The noble intention of the so called messengers of GODs, to unite people under ONE TRUE GOD failed to factor that, humans tend to be different from each other, both physiologically as well as mentally. At times, they may unite, for a cause or as some would say specific calling, but that unity will most likely not last, and will never translate into a permanent thing. That's how human beings are designed.

So there is probably no point in imposing, a specific version of one true GOD to every human being, because that probably goes against, how nature has designed, a human mind.

# Understanding Humans: Is the structure of the Society as we know it today under threat ?

Going by the daily news headlines, I believe, most of us have started to wonder if the global human society is heading in the right direction? It's not easy to see through the chaos and disruption. But this is not an accident, also accidents don't happen on their own just like that. There are always an underlying reason or reasons for any accident to have happened or occur. And it is by knowing the reasons that, we learn to understand the causes of an accident, as a way to help improve a system, whatever that might be.

My own view is that, in fact our society has been slowly sleep walking into whatever it is going through today. And going forward, there is a likelihood that, the current arrangement maybe falling apart, creating serious unrest. In other words, in the next 50-years, we may not have a society as we have come know it. This is no longer a radical thought, but a real possibility, and it's one of the reasons why, the rich and the famous are busy preparing for such eventuality, be it by buying a bunker or a remote island, or preparing to move to another planet. Who knows, they have probably lost faith in human resilience?

Having said that, maybe they understand well that, the current systems in place aren't working well at all. Most of us are used to two competing ideas around which we have organised the economies of various nation states. On one hand, we have a market driven approach, where we expect a free market to deliver peace and prosperity, but so far it hasn't. Then on the other hand, we have an approach which is quite similar to a religion. It tends to be quite tempting to start with, but always fails to deliver the end result aka the God, or in other words, forever peace and prosperity, in case of socialism.

While I do find myself favouring capitalism over socialism. Over time, I have also realised that like any infrastructure, capitalism has capacity problem. It isn't designed for unlimited growth or demand. For capitalism to be efficient, it needs an optimum level of demand. It can't serve everyone with the same quality forever. And it is one of the reasons why, more and more people living in capitalistic society are feeling left behind, while a very small percentage of the population in the same society continue to immensely benefit from the system. So to counter the increasing inequality and imbalance, some people are finding an extreme version of socialism quite tempting. And this tussle is one of the reasons for the society to rift further apart.

People are increasingly getting entrenched in their views, and electing leaders who they believe reflect not just their thinking, but also speaks for them. It is one of the reasons why leaders who tend to be on extreme right or left are getting elected or heard, because they seem to be speaking to a very willing audience. And those occupying a centrist position are the ones struggling to make sense of the ongoing chaos.

Leaders who lectured on social morality or ethics failed to recognise their shortcomings, by ignoring the warning signs, or sometimes simply playing the self righteous game. So there is enough blame to go around. The question is, do we let the society fall apart, or is there any way to make things better.

Being an optimistic, but also a realist, my own view on the subject matter is somewhat complicated. For example, contrary to the popular view, my mind is of the opinion that, leaders like Trump, as a side effect of their disruption, might have in fact bought us a bit more time, to solve the problem facing our society. I would take disruption and chaos over possible civil wars and unrest. The fight between extreme right and left will continue, and it should. We need to allow people to have their say. Even if, the leaders they choose will create turbulence. Criticism of their views will only be counterproductive. At least, that's my own view, and I have seen ample evidence, to be convinced that, it's more or less an accurate reflection of the society.

The winds will change directions, no matter what. If a product works only for 1% percent of the population then there is clearly an issue with that product. You cannot simply keep dismissing those 99%, who aren't seeing any benefit from capitalism as sore losers. Also the idea that, a society can get everything for free forever as championed by extreme socialism is quite simply a fantasy, and it goes against everything that the nature is. Everything in nature has a shelf life. And no system can last forever.

Inclusive progress isn't easy, as the idea of progress differs from people to people. The idea of organising large groups of humans living together while sharing a common bond, be it a nation state ; religion; language or culture, has worked so far, but it has also created rifts. There are increasing signs of divisions within similar culture, religion or nation for that matter. And as human population grows, so will the rifts.

So the obvious question then is, do we find a way to control the human population, or create a new narrative to condition the larger human society as a whole. And maybe the answer is yes to both. Not only that, the disruption and chaos is also an opportunity, to change the overall status quo. It makes sense, to look at ways to change the way we do global trade, or how our financial markets are currently designed.

Creating a new human civilisation on a different planet does increase the odds of the survival of the entire human species, but we also need to work harder, to preserve the species on earth while we have the chance to do so. The markets, religions or the nation states are all human ideas, and they will have to evolve with time. But not all transmission of change is seamless or smooth, so sometimes there will be turbulence and teething issues. Those who fly know that, turbulence is part and parcel of flying, and it can be quite scary and threatening at times. And people who can see the big picture will most likely end up making better investments decisions over time. That's also at play.

# 64 SUCCESS AND LUCK ....

# Understanding Humans: Success and luck

There are many theories around success, and how one could succeed. So to do our own discovery, I decided to work with our team at Nine (9) Visions. A company founded to understand human. We wanted to understand " SUCCESS " that most people chase. And in the process, we poured over all sorts of data covering a wide range of metrics including personalities; character; education ; network ; decision making abilities ; opportunities; leadership skills among others.

The team ran a simulation for 35 existing successful people, who are people of global repute. And compared them to others using the same metrics. I must say, I started out thinking " Success " is most likely a process powered by an algorithm, and we need to figure out if there is a common denominator or factor among those who we believe are successful or have succeeded. And after over 10 months of work, what we have found is that, while individuals do play a role in their success, the deciding factor however is, a common variable that we know as " luck ". I personally didn't agree with the findings, so I asked the team to go over our work again, but I am afraid whether I agree with it or not, it looks like luck is the deciding factor for the success of all the candidates we studied. So yes, you do need a bit of luck to succeed. I still have issues with this finding, but unless we have missed out something, the common factor among all the 35 candidates we rigorously studied seems to be what we would classify as LUCK. But yes, to sustain the success, you do need high quality skills. And it looks like, another team based in Italy has came to the same conclusion.

So maybe, luck is the common factor. And so now we want to understand " luck ", what exactly is luck. It will be an interesting journey. I personally held a view that " success " could possibly be a defined process powered by algorithm, and it probably is, and luck is an important element of that algorithm.

To summarise, all the elements play a role in the overall process and the equation or algorithm that we define as success, but the common variable is probably luck. And it's one of the common variable that our study has identified among the candidates we studied. Now with regards to luck, we don't really know what is luck, so I am assuming, it's probably a very important variable of the entire equation , and probably also an algorithm in itself. If we understand all this better then, we could map out a better road to success for our fellow humans, and train people, how to succeed with guaranteed results. That's the objective here.

To be classified as a scientist in the 16th century, all you had to do is read some science book, and in 18th century you probably needed to experiment in lab somewhere. And mostly because there was so much easy science to discover. But as we progressed, science became quite difficult, and the reason being, it became harder to do new discoveries. Having said that, we continue to discover new science, but some of these discoveries are down to pure accident or one could say chance. An equation is incomplete if, it fails to factor and account for all the variables, and I am now of the opinion that while writing the algorithm for success, one should factor in or account for luck also. This probably completes the process.

And while trying to figure out the variable " luck " in the overall algorithm based process known as " success ", I discovered the theory of randomness. In a way, "Luck " is quite an unpredictable variable, it follows no symmetrical pattern, in fact, there is no pattern, its random. But it's there. And I think the theory of randomness could possibly explain so many unexplainable things or events. If not for the random nature of evolution, we won't have so much diversity. Learning to factor and harness randomness, and most importantly accepting its role is, quite likely key to creating a successful and workable equation for " Success ".

65 THE ONE PERCENT...

# Understanding Humans: The one percent

The telescopes can see around 100 billion visible galaxies, but based on other estimates, there could be potentially over 3 trillion galaxies making up the entire system that, we know as the Universe. And in our own galaxy, there are over one billion estimated planets, and out of this, at least 100,000 planets could possibly be Earth like.

And using the hypothesis that life itself is an emergent phenomenon, and an intelligent life form is key to longevity of life. There are or were potentially over 100 million living species, of this around 1 million evolved into intelligent life. Within these 1 million intelligent life form, the evolution has probably designed provisions for possibly 1% of the entire population of a specific species, to not conform to any narrative or conditioning.

In short, these 1% are designed by evolution to be enablers. It's possible that, humans as species wouldn't have come about, without the 1% of the wandering and exploring chimps. And the same goes for other species. It is the 1% humans, who fail to conform to a narrative or overall conditioning that are, possibly the designed enablers or enabled soldiers who continue to help the human species evolve. And they could be scientists, explorers, leaders, social activists, humanitarians, or people who get tagged as messengers from a God.

# 66 THE TRAP...

# Understanding Humans: The TRAP

Evolutionary history of life on the planet that humans refer to as earth, goes back hundreds of millions of years. And we, the humans are the new arrivals on the scene, in the terms of the overall journey that life has done already so far. Every life form owes its existence to chance and probability, and all are powered by the technological process that we know as evolution. None of us had any say in our creation. Also most complex life forms, have to go through a journey of struggle while living. Again they have no say in it, and yes evolution has enabled these different life forms to deal with the struggles of living. But it's all about learning from a process of trial & error. So be it, an animal or a human, we all find a way to cope, and navigate our journey through the process that we have learnt to refer to as living.

Humans have devised their own ways and routines, to go about their process of living. Some live for a God, others for their goals and ambitions. In short, we tend to find a way and reason to live. And when we struggle then, we look to find solace in or through philosophy, poetry and other things that gives us comfort. Science is enabling us to dig a bit deeper and unravel the entire puzzle, in which we find ourselves. But still, there are too many unknowns. And sometimes, all this can get overwhelming for a human mind.

So you could be forgiven to conclude that, somehow we are all stuck in a trap of some sort, and there is probably no way out. But the question I ask myself everyday is, maybe there is a way out ? Maybe we could turn off the entire machine, but then there is a moral risk, as most of us would probably want to continue to experience their living, and rightly so. We are all participating in a circus, and we call that circus, the process of living. And there is no right or wrong way of living really. Those who live so they can go to heaven after their death as a reward from their Gods, or those like me, who know that a life is living through them, and their purpose or goals are all self created, in order to make it easier for them to live without going insane. We all have no choice, but to find a way to live, and in doing so also learn to enjoy the process.

The modern human society is continuing to find new ways, to keep the journey interesting. But then, there is always a small percentage, who continue their pursuit to unravel the puzzle. It's a very frustrating journey for those, who keep looking for answer. In fact, at times, it's quite a miserable way to exist, because the answers you are looking for isn't easy to come by. So sometimes, you do envy those, who have conditioned their minds to follow a religious narrative to explain their existence, and live following a set of rules.

There is no specific reason for a Universe or humans to exist, at least that's the answer I have to work with for now. Sometimes it may feel a bit unfair that the process of living has so much struggle, and it's not right or proper that evolution keeps creating complex life forms, only so they can exist, and in doing so go through the struggles of living. If a God designed such a system then, I am afraid, it's quite a sadistic system. Is it not ? But I personally don't feel it has anything to do with a God at all. It's probably time, we broke away the shackles, and found a new way to help us unravel this puzzle.

Let's take tailor made complex life forms with inbuilt ability to survive in most environments across the Universe, and while we are at it, let's also attempt to build the Universe with the existing building blocks that are in abundance.
A journey towards being limitless sounds more liberating to me then, following half baked narratives, and in the process also learn to hate and kill my own fellow humans. I hope one day, we will get out of this trap.

# 67 BEING AN ENTREPRENEUR ...

# Understanding Humans: Being an entrepreneur

The modern society won't be what it is today without entrepreneurs and their enterprise. And we all know that. But do we know what it takes to be an entrepreneur, and what is being an entrepreneur anyways ? Also is there a perfect process to help people navigate their way to an entrepreneurial success? And most importantly, why is all this relevant at all ? After all, everyone is different, and what works for me, may or may not work for others. Having said that, we all learn from our experience. And sharing our experience is, one way of sharing our knowledge also. That's how the human society has evolved over time.

We all celebrate successful entrepreneurs, and probably rightly so, but the road on which an entrepreneur has to travel is quite topsy-turvy. And not all make it. A big part of being an entrepreneur is about constant learning, and developing skills, most important of all, the ability to make right decisions and finding ways to be more productive, or else you may struggle to pay for your living.

If you are learning to hustle then, it's worth knowing that, the idea of chasing deals, or doing a set amount of meetings or networking every day or each month isn't an automatic ladder to success. In fact, in most cases it doesn't work. Also you can't read your way to success. It is about learning from trial & error. So one has to learn to make better and right decisions on what is worth spending your time and resources over, and what isn't.

Also doing constant networking doesn't really help, instead one should focus on developing existing relationships, and creating new opportunities through the tested network, to avoid time wastage. It is important to develop a network that is on the same page and wavelength with you.

People working for institutions are salaried employees, and they get paid to do a lot of meetings. And while they maybe stretched, their overall productivity or output from these meetings remains quite low. A very sizeable numbers of the meetings can be done through or over phone calls or e-mails. And entrepreneur especially those starting out, don't have the luxury or comfort of collecting a pay cheque come what may.

Therefore, it is not about the amount of meetings, but about the quality of meetings and networking. Also one should focus on a common destination, in other words, develop the ability to create a shared and common goal, whereby people can buy into and also share your overall vision. It is never about my way or no other way. You can't make it without others, being a self made requires others to build you. Getting people to trust you takes time, and not all will.

Building a business relationship is like any other human relationship. It takes time and requires commitment. And not all relationships will succeed. Yes a business school can teach you a process, but in the end, a large part of how you build your business is dependent on your own ability to understand human beings, and also being able to navigate your way through. And then learning, how to get people on board especially those who can help you with building a momentum around whatever it is that you are trying to achieve.

If you are an entrepreneur with an amazing idea, you do need to realise that, not all brilliant ideas get funded. Most of the time, people won't see what may you be looking at, in terms of potential. People commit capital based on their expectations and overall perception. Therefore not all prospects you date will end up in a lasting marriage. And most importantly, not all capital is the right capital. Also, it isn't easy to know who may be wasting your time, and who isn't. So you will need to learn to see through the conversations and discussion, and then make your own conclusions. One size fits all isn't a strategy, at best it's a lazy approach.

Don't forget, you are dealing with humans, and human factors will influence your end result. You may do ten meetings a day, and not have anything worth showing. So your productivity will remain volatile, in terms of your ability to get desired results from a potential meeting, especially if you are linking your effort to a positive outcome.

In the end, being an entrepreneur is quite lonely, so it is about you, and sometimes nothing you will try, will work, and you will have to try again without any guarantees. Not all succeed. But the process does help you learn, and that type of learning can't be taught in a business school. It's not all glory and sunshine, there are many dark alleys through which you will have to go through, and you will have to learn to be your best hope.

Nobody can teach you how to succeed, sometimes those trying teach you how to succeed are the ones struggling.

And knowing that you can't possibly know everything is the best advice you can give yourself. It is a long journey, so those who do try to sprint their way to success, do end up running out of steam. Also, it is not just about succeeding, but being able to sustain that success, by learning to continuously evolve and staying ahead. Or you may lose whatever you had, and it won't be easy to come back. It is not for everyone especially those used to stability and certainty, or those looking for work-life balance, but then no job comes with a permanent guarantee either.

And remember, People will only celebrate your failures, if they are convinced that you did succeed in the end.

# 68 RELIGION AND SCIENCE ...

# Understanding Humans : Religion & Science

So the question is, what is religion and science? My initial view on religion was that, it is a belief system, but that view over time did change, as my own understanding of religion and science evolved.

Today my mind understands religion as an ideology. Because simply put, religion is collection of ideas and ideals. At the time when, our ancestors didn't know how to use science to test or verify the ideas they conceived through their imagination, as a way to understand their existence and the big picture. And therefore, people had no real alternatives but to take those ideas at the face value, and over time somehow, it became easier for people to assume that, those ideas as knowledge came directly from a divine, in other words, possibly a God, who speaks through a selected few. And then some people took those ideas further to compile them into religious literatures.

That process, most probably kick started the advent of religious practices. However, today we have learnt to take science for granted, and it is in fact, a verifiable belief system, which religion is not. Religion proposes that one should trust and have a belief in the preachings of a religion, but you can never really verify or validate any of the ideas or ideals. Because by design religion fails to offer a solution on verification. Whereas science offers just that. So in a way science is a technical upgrade to our original pursuit of finding out who we are. For example, we learn to believe in gravity, because through science we can verify that gravity exists, and also create it. With the help of science, we have learnt to harness nature and also learn from it, and in doing so, managed to fast track our development.

Religion proposes various hypothesis and theories, but it fails to go beyond that. But through science we have the ability to either validate or disapprove these theories. Some of the ideas proposed by religion has indeed helped built the core principles of modern day humanity, and one could argue that, humanity is evolving as a better version of religion. The reason being, humanity seems to work better with the modern day human society, and the core principles of humanity will continue to evolve with the society. So it is not a rigid system.

Religion as a tool has served humanity well, but some of the ideas and ideals of religion will need to be upgraded, if it is to continue serving the society. I have learnt to realise that, It is not about science vs religion, in fact science comes as an upgrade to our pursuit of God, simply because it has the ability to helps us verify our imagination of a potential God. Also we need to take a bit of risk, and reimagine God. A collaborative effort is required. With the help of science, we could bin the theories and ideas that can't be verified to be true, and move on to the next one, until we get closer to a possible answer. And who knows through a process of elimination, we could potentially find a way to not only describe, but also verify a God like entity. And that's the journey worth doing, instead of continuing with the narrative to no where.

# 69 THE HUMANS..

# Understanding HUMANS : The Humans

As humans, we are a by—product of the evolutionary history of Life. We were conceived, created and designed on a system that we have learnt to call Earth. And without a strong input from the Sun, we will most likely be not around. Our history was unplanned, and there is no evidence to conclude that somehow, we are going to sail smoothly into a future that we have designed for ourselves. There was, and there is no plan, is there ?

All of us are busy living, and some of us live with a hope that a God will guide us all into whatever that future might be. So we are serving a god. And we do find something or the other, to keep us busy. That's the big picture. But what we don't always factor is, how the internal time clock within our cells and the gene clock that controls the evolution of a human brain are all, playing a role in writing the past, present and future of the human story. Our ancestors worshipped Sun, because they somehow knew that our survival is thanks to that mighty Sun shinning bright in the Sky. The science we know tell us that, a different Sun could have created a different outcome. And where we are today as a species is, directly and indirectly related to our actions and inactions in the past. Who would have known that a simple addiction to tea will indirectly enable a country like England to create a mighty empire. It is tea that helped prevent water borne illnesses, helping the population boom in the country. Addiction to caffeine across Europe made Europeans plan revolution, and change their society.

The greed of the Europeans to make profit from trade especially caffeine and metal ended up repopulating humans across various parts of Earth. And a large part of our history is basically, humans doing what they thought was right for them at the time. There was no collective humanity as such. And whether we like it or not, but we are all interconnected. Our past has happened, and it has helped shape our present. And whatever we may think of it, without a strategy for the progress of collective humanity, we as species may not survive. We fight over our culture, religion etc without knowing that, in fact we weren't born with them. It was simply passed on to us, and we took them on, because that's how we are conditioned.

Science tells us that, our early experience can change our DNA. And I sincerely hope that, we work towards creating a future where our historical baggage isn't passed on to our next generation. We are designed to survive on a system like Earth, and in a way, it is written in our DNA. So to live in a different star system, we will most likely have to evolve into something that we are not today.

But the question I ask myself is, while we should rightly focus on the future, let us not forget that in our immediate present, some of us are still living as a beast. Exploiting our own, killing our own, and carrying hatred without ever trying to understand our common evolutionary history. The trillions of cells that make us, are the same, they don't hate each other. Imagine, if they did? The sun that powers us, does that regardless. And the earth that is nurturing us, has no care for our hatred for each other. We are all designed in the same way, to live and experiencing living. And I have learnt to admire those of us, who have found a way to think of our collective future. I am relevant only because of others. And that's how it is.

# 70  SIMPLE AND COMPLEX .....

# Understanding Humans: Simple and complex

Simplicity comes from something simple, but so does complexity. The same simple principles or rules that create simplicity also creates complexity. Using basic elements evolution has learnt to create complex beings such as humans over time. And somehow evolution managed to master the process, after a period of trial & error.

Evolution through, what I tend to describe as algorithm, figured out what works. And then used that, to create complexities that we see around us. So what is simple is also complex at the same time. Uncertainty and unpredictability is hard wired in the overall design of the universe. A simple inanimate object can be responsible for creating complexities. Chaos and uncertainty are key ingredients on which evolution has built everything around us. So a possible future will always remain uncertain, because that's the true nature of evolution. A simple person will also be complex at the same time, because that's how they are probably wired and designed.

We keep looking for similarities, because the principle of self-similarity is how nature has built complex things. That's how coastlines and rocks across the world look the same. You don't need a complex God to conceive complexities, it is the simplicity that overtime creates complexities. Praying does not provide answers, it is the fear of uncertainty that overwhelms us. A God or the Universe isn't testing a human. Chaos and uncertainty is inherent to how the system is designed.

# 71  THE NARRATIVE.....

# Understanding humans: The narrative

The most established and common religious narrative is based around an idea of a just God, who supposedly decided to create humans, possibly out of love. But without ever bothering to seek their permission, and also never consulting with the humans, on how and when their lives will be terminated.

Religion has tried to explain all that using the narrative, commonly known as a God's will. And overtime humans were conditioned, to not only buy into that narrative, but also seek salvation from the cycle of life and death, by a way of worshipping a God. In a way, that is learning what living is or possibly could be, from a religion's perspective.

But the question worth asking is, why would a just and wise God conceive an idea that seems quite unjust. Doesn't it? Also why would a just and wise God or the universe for that matter, knowingly trap humans into a cycle of life and death, and then somehow decide to reward them for their deeds. And to mention, keep pulling the string, just to make sure that humans continue to praise and worship that God. Are we missing something?

Sometimes, I do wonder, is this all a reality show produced and directed by a just God? To me, this idea resembles enslavement, as humans know it better, and there is a sad human history of slave trade. This description of a  God like figure, shows limits of a human imagination.

I would argue that, humans are a product of chance and probability, powered by evolution. At best the human species is probably just a side show. The existence of humans is all down to the technological process that's known as evolution, and not because of a deliberate decision made by a God to create humans out of love, and then build the entire universe for them. This thinking, however tempting, is most likely, a product of human imagination, where humans obviously take precedent over everything else. However humans aren't as old as the universe, are they ?Human made ideologies have enslaved humans, as evident from most of their ideas, be it religion; nation state; economy ; money ; culture among others. So it is humans who enslaved humans or other living beings. And a God or the Universe isn't pulling strings, just so humans can fear or continuously worship it.  Again, the construct of the idea most probably comes from human imagination.

Humans find a reason to love, live and hope, and they also find reason to lose hope or the desire to live. Evolution has enabled humans to tailor their own evolutionary journey, so it's up to humans to chart out their journey going forward. And this is why understanding Humans is key to try to project where the human species may end up.

## Time for a BREAK ?

Hope " Understanding Humans " was a good read. I wrote them as part of my own self discovery. We are a complex species, and understanding a human being, requires undergoing and in the process understanding the overall human journey. It is only by living that, we get better at living.

I am quite curious if, you were able to relate to them? And if you did then, please do jot down your thoughts on the empty page.  To continue reading, please turn to the next page.

And continuing with our experiment, we are now going back to the  Poems or whatever you would like to call them.

Thank you ....

NEXT PAGE ........

72 POEMS.....

# 73 IN A TRANCE .....

## In a Trance...

The mind I was
Felt sad and numb
Nothing it could think of
Was going to make
Living more fun

But was I hurt
Or lost on the way
Of that I had no sense

I could see the sun
Burn and burn
And the warmth
It radiated helped
All lives walk and run

Looking at the sunsets
From the shores
Living was still as
Mundane as doing
The daily chores

Stories and Fantasies that
I was Once told, about that
Now my mind isn't sure

I exist because I have to
And I wake up everyday
Because that is what life wants to

I chase no glory nor the gods
I find myself existing

In this vast universe
Against all the odds

My eyes are not
On any prize and this
Goes against all
The good advice

All the drama is old
And I have no interest
In galore or the gold

Do I care about anything
Not even my own life
I ask this of myself now
Almost everyday twice

Wind blows and
I could see it
Shaking up the trees
Moving the dirt with it
As it would please

Answers to what I seek
Is still out of my reach
Even when I deep dive
Into my imagination
My understanding is weak

Is this all a game
To me now, it is
All the same

I am in it
And I know

There is also
An end to it

If the universe
Came from nothing
And it has no plans

I wonder if I have
Put myself into a trance

74 RULES ...

# Rules...

It wasn't meant to be, they said
What is meant to be, will be
That is how, we learn to be

We learn to wait, for a date
With our destiny and fate

What is in my destiny or my fate
Am I deserving, or am I late
This is the narrative
Served up on our plate

And when the life that
We are all living is at stake
Is then that we hope, there is a god
Writing a good story on our slate

I was told, a God wrote the show
Making humans the centre of attraction
And in it, living was full of distraction

The road of travel
Was governed by the rules
Which later became the tools
For manipulation, and help others rule

# 75 MYSTERY...

## Mystery...

Play me a song
That takes me away
To a place, but where
I won't say

Me with me
On a journey
Just to be

Melodies, sweet and sour
Ringing through my veins

I will remember
Not to look back
On what I once was

There is no place
For me to call home
Or gravity to hold me back

I love the free fall
Knowing there is
Nobody to call

Maybe that's how
I will learn to walk tall
Before I fall

The eyes are shut
But the mind can see

Going through the
Memory of what was me

Nature is what
I know created me
And to nature is where
I will go back

Come dance with me
Till the end of me
And let me pass away
Into the mystery

# 76 MEMORIES....

Memories....


Memories of me
Are all inside of me
Sometimes they flow
Quite wild and free

Some rain on me
And some try
To set me free

That is how
It has been

What will be, will be
I may drown in the sea
Or learn to crawl
On my knees

How would you
Ever know how
Have I been

Sometimes I have seen
The world could be mean

I can hear what
You won't say
Your soul my dear
Can still be saved

Come here and
Let me hear
The sound of
Your heartbeat

Yes, it is ok
To feel the pain

Let the memories rain
And wet your feet
You see, Life is at play
So just take your seat

# 77 BEING FREE....

## Being Free ...

I am the air
That I breath
The smile that I wear
Even when others
Would only look
And stare in despair

I go up and
Down the ladder
Of all possible
Emotions and flare

Disregard me, if you
Can not regard me
Disobedience is also
Sometimes quite fair

We may or may not agree
To dance, cry or just weep
As some would say
Life is never sweet

My tradition is

In being untraditional
And my culture will
Never be used
As a vulture
To prey on the weak
So I can strive in
Whatever it is that I seek

I wish I was free
But I don't yet know
What it is, to be free

Freedom of a human
To be free from humans
And why is it that
One has to die
To be able to
Rest in peace

So I wonder if
I'll ever be free

The world will continue
To define me as it sees

Maybe I'll never know
What it is, to be truly free

# 78 BEING NO MORE...

# Being no more...


I am sleeping
On your floor
Telling you my story
And much more

Undressing what was
Once quite raw

I have been sleeping over it
And stopping it to grow

Listening to all
The songs I could store

And one by one, they all
Start to throw me
To a place
That is no more

Story of a journey
Now left behind

How I wish
I could unwind

What used to be
Is now of
No use to me at all

The melody of old
Seems to have
Lost it's hold

I am at peace at last
But who knows
This may not last

One day I will
Go back to sleep
And promise me
You won't weep

The Stars will die and fall
From the sky above, that's all
No body to grieve over them
Or remember their name to call

I will tell you more
But the mind I am
Wants to soar
And be lost
To the magic
Of being no more

# 79 CARRY THE DAY ...

Carry the day..


When there is
Nothing left to say
And nothing you
Would want to
Put on display

Yet carry on with
The show is also
Your only way

A life has no
Less or more meaning
Even if it is
Not on display

Say what you
Would want to say
Not how others
May want you to play

The plight of
A human life
May at times
Feel in a disarray

But don't forget
A human's hope
Is also that ray
That can carry the day

Just learn to be
With yourself all the way
And that is what I feel
Your Gods may also say

# 80 COME WITH ME ...

## Come with me...


Come with me
And let me show you
What your world could be

Be lost to yourself
So you can find
Who and what you could be

We are not made to last
And our stories
No matter what
Will always come to pass

I am living and so you are
And there will come a time
When our perspectives
Will be far apart
And it may feel as if
whatever we were, and had is
Being lost to the dark

We not may be able to
See each other's world
Through the same glass

We are only humans after all
At times we all stumble and fall

When you can't run
I hope you will
Find a way to crawl

Sometimes there is
No escape or rescue
And that is when your
Love for yourself comes due

Your hope is you
And so is your God

Keep going for
As long as you can last

Be your friend until the end
And a messenger that
Your God sent

You will find a new friend in you
Who will make you into a new you

Learn to love who you are
Even when you feel
That your world is drifting far

I wrote this for you
Just incase I am not
In that world where you are

# 81 NO MORE ...

## No More ..

Deleting myself away I was
The memories of
Whoever I thought
I once was

Letting go of what
Was my own show
Unwinding the journey of old

The stories that I wrote
And also those that I was told

I wouldn't hold on to anything
Pain or the fear
And whatever else
That I ever held dear

There were times when
Whatever was I
Got in the way of life

A life was living
Through me, now I know

The air was me and
So was the water

It is people who
Made me important
They were a reason
For my joy and the pain

Even when I felt my life
Was going down the drain

The peace that I always sought
Was inside me
And so was the happiness
Worth more than any gold

My friends and my foes
Are now all left behind
As the life I was once
Starts to unwind

The journey of my existence
Is now being unfold
And the mind that I once was
Is now, no more

82 I ....

I....


There I was
Wandering somewhere
Inside a mind
A situation that
Can't be easily explained or defined

I couldn't tell if
I was that thought
Or the thought
Somehow derived from a mind
That was my probably mine

What I am or
What I live for
Remains an unresolved puzzle
Inside my mind

Living is what
I have learnt to do
And existing is
What I still am

Capturing the moments
As memories of
The journey I have had
Some good and some bad

Stories of Me
I won't tell
Even if I felt
I was in hell

Why I ask, why
I have to pry
Into the affairs
Of my own mind

They say, there is a divine
And you will be fine
But fine is not
What my mind
Wants to be

Who and What is I
Still remains a mystery

What I write or say
May one day become
Part of my history

A history of me
I wouldn't write
But that is what
I feel may survive

# 83 UNKNOWN...

Unknown ....


I tried to save humanity
But little did I know
That it was me
Who needed saving

Humans were busy living
And their humanity
At times went missing

I lived knowing
I will die
I always wanted the pie
That I thought was life

It was good to be alive
Even when it felt
It may all be a lie

To love and be loved
Was roll of a dice

I was never shy
To fall for the sky

The stars above me
Were my pilgrimage
Shining bright as my guide

My imaginations were lit
And so was the life

Mysterious and alive is
How I felt

And that's how
The mystery began, they said

Save myself now I won't
I will willingly dive
Into the unknown

It is as unknown
How I was born
And unknown is
How I may want to be known

# 84 IMAGINATION AT WORK...

## Imagination at Work....

Soaring high above the sky, I was
Removed from the world
As I flew past the rubble and the rust

My place in the world
Was inside my mind
And so was the world

The peace and serenity
Along with the life
That I had learnt to love

People made living interesting
Yet it is people who I thought
Somehow made things worst

Nations and organised societies
Gods, religions and money
Over time all became a curse

And all of it were
A product of
Imagination at work

## Time for a BREAK ?

Hope you enjoyed the poems along with the experiment. And now, we have come to the end of this journey titled " Journey of a human mind ".I wish that your journey continues. And before I leave you. I thought, I will take the liberty and insert a short story titled " the star people " along with a note " the castle ", "change ' and " reimagining God " under imagination@Work.

And that will be it from me. Hopefully, we will get a chance to connect someday, and talk about our journeys. My best wishes to you, and thank so much for your time.

Live on, and carry on investing in yourself. It is the best investment that you will ever make.

Thank you ....

# 85 IMAGINATION @WORK - THE STAR PEOPLE

# A short story: The star people

765,000 years in the future, on a far away star system, a species is trying to trace back its origin. They are an extremely advance civilisation with ability to do interstellar travels as a matter of routine. The species has also mastered the process of resurrecting individuals, by a way of downloading people's mind and consciousness on to new bodies. And that's how they also reproduce.

They refer to themselves as the star people. Not only because they have learnt to harness the power of stars, but also because they can create stars. And as star people, they have built star Systems, and also a home for themselves spread across the universe. They have a lot going for them, but among them, there are those who have a nostalgia for their past.

A group among them that calls itself historians, are always looking for clues, to help them trace back their history. And after searching for years, somehow by accident they bump into a structure that, they previously believed was an ordinary natural system. But after studying the entire system. They realised, it isn't, and therefore it was created by someone. That discovery changed their thought process.

Star people as civilisation then made a conscious decision to trace back their own history. And when they were close to giving up, the reality started unraveling quite rapidly. They discovered that, star people are in fact a direct offspring of what used to be a dominant species on a planetary system called Earth. This dominant species used to call themselves Humans, and it is the humans who genetically engineered a new breed of humans, who over time went on to become the star people.

Humans and the hybrids, as star people were referred to by humans, couldn't get along. So a decision was made, to move the star people to a new system. And overtime, the disconnect grew, and star people decided to move on. In the process, the origin of their history got lost. Hybrids aka the star people started their evolutionary journey as the upgraded offsprings of humans, and like humans, they continued to question their existence.

As advanced civilisation, they cracked mortality, became an interstellar species, but they couldn't completely disconnect from the  human elements that made them. They realised, it is death that made a human life beautiful. Although humans feared death, but death in fact was their greatest enabler. Star people could  live forever by continuously downloading themselves onto to new bodies, but they started longing for the life of a human. Which humans at the time thought was at best imperfect.

# 86 IMAGINATION @WORK - THE CASTLE

# A short note - the castle

I built a castle, but never lived in it. A dream that I conceived, but never lived it. And they said, what are you talking about, are you mad?

And mad, I maybe I said " a man about dreams ". Dream I must, everyday of the week, of a world where we are all mad about being there for each other.

I won't be alive, to live the dream or cherish the castle that ,I would like to build for my own kind, but try I will anyways.

# 87 IMAGINATION @WORK - CHANGE....

# Change

You may want to change the world, but in the process, the world might change you. Imagine, if the world was to end in the next hour then, what would you do ? As I see it, we make our own realities, and with it, our own world. And the way we see our world reflects who we are, or what we are becoming. I don't know, is in a way, also knowing that we don't know, so therefore even in not knowing, we know enough to know that, we don't know. At times, preaching is not what we need. I feel that, it is by sharing our own journeys through the process of self discovery, we can provide a different and unique perspective to others, thereby creating a reference pool. In other words, a working reference manual on understanding humans and living. A God is hope to some, and to some, the answers to all their questions. We all share the same world, but within that world, we have also created our own world. Haven't we ? And when our own world is not in sync with the world that others have created, it is then that, we see conflict. So maybe, when you get tempted to change the world, you might want to ask yourself if, it is your own world that you need to change?

# 88 IMAGINATION @WORK - REIMAGINING A GOD...

# Reimagining a God

So in my imagination I am trying to talk with god, but for some reason my imagination keeps failing me, as I am unable to imagine a potential God. It's quite possible that, it is because of the conditioning I have went through. And therefore my mind today isn't able or probably to some extent incapable of conceiving or imagining a God that falls outside of the description or narrative of a mainstream religion.

All the construct of my imagination so far, somehow ends up imagining a god that carries a resemblance of a God, as described by religion. I guess, I will have to concede that, I will most likely keep trying and failing. And it will be interesting to see where I end up in the process. The mission is to reimagine a god that is outside of the existing religious description of a potential God.

The question is , if a God exists then, why does that God exist ? And also, who created that God, and why ? If something created a God then, who or what created that something ? This is a classic God paradox in my view, isn't it ? Taking this thought process further. Assuming a God exist then, what was the need for the God to create anything ? And why should a God's creation be thankful to a God for creating them, especially when that God didn't seek their prior permission. Also using a working assumption that sometimes a god does like to test its creation especially humans, and if that's true then, why should a god test its creations ? And why should the god's creation be at the mercy of that God's will or intention ? If a God knows what is best for its creation then, why can't the God, let it be known?

One way to look at this entire puzzle will be, to start with an understanding that, a god probably only exist, because the creations exist already. And therefore without its creation, a god most likely won't exist . So in other words, a god is only relevant because of its creation. Then what is a god potentially? Could it be, just an idea, or an entity, a process, a complex system like the universe, an operating system, an extremely sophisticated self learning and evolving algorithm based intelligent process or system, the core ingredient or the building block of life itself? Or is it an invention of a human mind, as a way to explain away complex issues ? It's not an easy question to answer, but by continuing to explore various possibilities, we may come close to a common and acceptable explanation one day.

The question is, will the world stop existing if, for example humans stopped worshipping or believing in a god or the idea of a God ?. Most likely not, as there are no reason to assume that, the world may end without a god. God is quite clearly a complex subject, and the easiest answers one could think of is, yes a god exist, but what we can't explain is why or what it is. Or no a god doesn't exist, and in that case, there is no need to find answers to the question of God. And this is how we have conditioned ourselves. But maybe, it's time, we took a bit of risk, and gave our minds the freedom to explore all possible answers. And we could do this by putting our imagination to work.

Religion has so far anchored the idea and belief of the existence of a God, and it provides a construct of what that God might be, and also what it may want. And in doing so, it has also limited the definition of a possible god to a certain extent. The narrative has therefore been limited to following a god or the god's will. I feel that, it's probably time, we allowed our imagination to reimagine a god, and let's see what it comes up with ?

Imagine waking up in a place where you are the only human left alive, and you have no memory or recollection of who and what you are, it's like your mind has been wiped clean, but you are still conscious. The natural design of the mind is such that, it will start imagining. And when you are in that situation then, it's quite possible to imagine, how a human brain could have possibly conceived an idea that a supremely powerful entity like God might have created the entire living species and everything else with it. And since you happen to be out of the food chain, it's not difficult to conclude also that, somehow a god favoured you over other primitive creatures, and it may have created everything just for you, out of love. It is an entirely plausible assumption, but yes, we can't really conclude that, it is an accurate reflection of reality.

THIS PAGE IS LEFT EMPTY FOR YOUR NOTES

WISDOM FROM MY IMAGINARY GRANDMA:


Your ENEMIES are a PRODUCT of your CIRCUMSTANCES and of your own creation. You were not BORN with them, no body ever is. AND YOU won't take THEM with YOU ,when you are GONE.
It's HOW you DEAL with YOUR CIRCUMSTANCES that will DEFINE you, and not your ENEMIES.

## MORE WISDOM FROM MY IMAGINARY GRANDMA:

No one is ever born with experience or a manual on how to live a human life, yet somehow, by a way of living, we do find a way to live a life, and in the process, experience living. And doing so, become a reference to others.

SOME MORE WISDOM FROM MY IMAGINARY GRANDMA:

Love comes naturally to us, and so does hate. But what we choose, decides
what will become of us. Being good is a choice, and so is being bad. And
it's the choices that we make, makes us, who we are.

AND SOME MORE WISDOM FROM MY IMAGINARY GRANDMA:

Eyes don't see and appreciate beauty, a mind does. Based on its own understanding of what is beauty. And this understanding comes from, how a mind is conditioned.

# ABOUT THE AUTHOR

A human mind on a journey. Powered by imagination and driven by curiosity to learn and find the answers to many unanswered questions. And besides boring his friends and colleagues, by regularly sharing the endless social media posts on a range of issues. Sanjeev Kumar is also a Director & CEO at the Delamore & Owl Group Of Companies and the founder of DTM GLOBAL HOLDINGS LTD.

He is a market-seasoned professional and the recipient of " South East Asia Young Achiever's Award "
He is also the founder of Imagination@WORK and several other initiatives including of 9VISIONS and minds@WORK. Sanjeev holds a dual masters degree in Finance and commerce and also has an MBA.

As the CEO of the D&O group, he overseas business activities of the group in many different countries, and is a regular contributor on platforms that are helping shape the future of the financial market and the global business

# SOCIAL MEDIA CONNECTION WITH THE AUTHOR

twitter:@ S_K76
Facebook: www.facebook.com/personal.sanjeev
blog: www.sonykumar.com
Instagram: sk_human_being

( I am leaving the last few pages empty, because it's only on an empty page that you can write something magical and beautiful. If you want to write something or note down a  thought that pops into your mind then, please do )

Next page...

Next page...

THANK YOU.....

SEE YOU AROUND ……..

Hope you it was a good read!

*Sanjeev Kumar*

The end .......but the journey continues

11823492R00180

Printed in Great Britain
by Amazon